Short Walks in
Lincolnshire
and the Wolds

Guide to 20 easy walks of 3 hours or less

Published by Collins
An imprint of HarperCollins Publishers
Westerhill Road
Bishopbriggs
Glasgow G64 2QT

www.harpercollins.co.uk

First edition 2011

ISBN 978 0 00 739542 2

email: roadcheck@harpercollins.co.uk

Contents

Introduction

Walking near Caistor

Walking in Lincolnshire and the Wolds

For those who love wide open landscapes where you can see for mile upon mile; for those who are captivated by huge flocks of birds as they wheel overhead in the impossibly huge skies before they land en masse along the coastal flats; Lincolnshire is the place to be. It really is a world away from everyday life; an area of unexpected beauty and drama.

This large rural county, dominated by agriculture, is the second largest English county after Yorkshire. It is also one of the least populated; the countryside evokes an England of an era long gone, where the countryside of gently rolling hills and small wooded valleys, farmland bisected by hedgerows, drainage ditches and lanes, marshes, fenland and heathland, all allow the walker to enjoy a variety of different landscapes. You really do feel like you have left the hustle and bustle of everyday life behind and entered a more tranquil time and place. The scattering of small market towns and villages, often built from the local stone, give the county a welcoming feel. You won't get really challenging walks in this area, they are gentle and so are ideal for all abilities, but you do get a sense of 'getting away from it all' which really does lift the spirits. In many areas within Lincolnshire, particularly in the flatter land to the south, the sky dominates, and our varying English weather gives the scenery another dimension as you watch the ever-changing clouds roll in, their shadows scudding across the fields.

Walking is a pastime which can fulfil the needs of everyone. You can adapt it to suit your own preferences and it is one of the healthiest of activities. This guide is for those who just want to walk a few miles. It really doesn't take long to find yourself in some lovely countryside. All the walks are five miles or less so should easily be completed in under three hours. Walking can be anything from an individual pastime to a family stroll, or maybe a group of friends enjoying the fresh air and open spaces of our countryside. There is no need for walking to be competitive and, to get the most from a walk, it shouldn't be regarded simply as a means of covering a given distance in the shortest possible time.

The Lincolnshire Landscape

This huge county has some distinctive landscapes, many of which are very much the product of the hand of man. Large parts of the county are low lying; in fact three-quarters of it lies below 100ft (30m). Since Roman times man has reclaimed, drained and worked the land, creating today's agricultural landscape with its large fields, divided by hedgerows and lanes, and in the southern fenlands, where some of the land is below sea level, there are waterways, drainage channels and ditches. This southern area is very like the Netherlands and as a consequence it is sometimes known as South Holland.

The highest point in the county at 551ft (168m), is Wolds Top, situated near Normanby-le-Wold in the chalk uplands of the Lincolnshire Wolds. Although it is not particularly high in the scheme of things, it feels much higher than it is due purely to the fact that so much of the county is low lying. From this viewpoint you can get some spectacular views on a clear day; you may be able to see Lincoln Cathedral to the southwest and the Boston Stump to the southeast. Lincoln city is itself perched on a hill – the Lincolnshire Edge – a limestone ridge which commands superb views of the surrounding countryside.

Geology

Although the landscape has been modified considerably by man the basic shape of the land we see today is very much a product of the underlying geology. There is a series of hard and soft rocks which run roughly north to south and dip to the east. Over time, gradual weathering of the landscape by water, ice and wind has resulted in uneven erosion leaving two prominent upland areas divided by wide lowland strips. To the west of the county is the Vale of Trent which is mainly comprised of Lower Jurassic clays dating from about 195 million years ago. These relatively soft rocks are easily worn away and so form the low lying Vale. To the east of this is the Lincolnshire Edge which is a narrow, steep-sided limestone escarpment of extremely resistant rock dating from later

Countryside between Belchford and Scamblesby

Jurassic times. Separated from the Edge by a clay lowland area are the Lincolnshire Wolds, comprised mainly of Cretaceous chalk laid down under a warm sub-tropical sea 90 million years ago. The chalk is made up of microscopic marine creatures and you may also find fossil sea urchins and oysters in the rock as well as flint nodules. Some of these Jurassic and Cretaceous rocks which form the bones of the landscape have been hidden beneath younger deposits laid down during the Quaternary period when, during the Ice Age, the county was covered by a series of advancing and retreating ice sheets. The ice scoured the harder rocks and also deposited glacial tills. The Ice Age comprised a series of glacial advances broken by interglacial periods. During one of these phases – the Ipswichian Interglacial – the sea level rose due to the ice melt and the eastern part of the county was under the sea, this resulted in the eastern side of the chalk Wolds being cut back by the sea, creating coastal cliffs which are now stranded far inland several miles from the coast. Then, as recently as 10,000 years ago, after the final ice retreated the sea rose once again and marine sediments were deposited along the coast forming the flat coastal landscape and the Fens.

Wildlife in Lincolnshire

This rural county is rich in wildlife and has numerous nature reserves. Gibraltar Point to the south of Skegness includes a range of coastal habitats such as extensive dunes and both saltwater and freshwater areas. There is a visitor centre, hides and a network of paths along which you can explore the reserve. Plants you may see include the rare marsh orchid plus the colourful yellow flag iris. But it is the birdlife for which the reserve is rightly recognized. Redshank, ringed plover and lapwing breed at the reserve and it is also an important over-wintering, feeding, roosting and resting area where vast numbers of birds, both waterfowl and other migratory species such as swallows, can be seen during the autumn and winter months. The RSPB reserve at Freiston Shore near Boston is also worth a visit. You may see thousands of birds in the saltwater lagoon including avocets, redshanks and brent geese.

Donna Nook, just to the north of North Somercotes, is home to a colony of grey seals; it is also an RAF bombing range. Curiously, the seals seem comfortable with their noisy neighbours and get on happily with their daily lives. The best time to visit is November and December when the seals come ashore to give birth on the salt flats. To ensure they remain undisturbed, which is particularly important at breeding time, visitors are kept away from the seals by fencing, so it's worth taking a pair of binoculars in order to get a good view.

As well as the more open limestone areas, where wild flowers are in abundance in the spring and summer, there are also small pockets of mature woods; there is also quite a bit of ongoing tree and hedge planting in the county. One star tree in the county is the Bowthorpe Oak in Manthorpe near Bourne. This tree is reckoned to be over 1000 years old and has a circumference of almost 40ft (12m 30cm). Back in 1768 the massive hollow tree had a door added and seats fitted inside where 13 people could sit down to dine or, at a squeeze, 39 could stand. Some of the local children have an annual tea and treat inside the tree. It is on a private farm so the oak is home to sheep and chickens for most of the year.

History

The county underwent extensive settlement during the Roman occupation. Ermine Street (now the A15) followed the line of the Lincolnshire Edge, meeting the Fosse Way (now the A46) at Lincoln. Lincoln itself is a Roman town (Lindum) and once served as a fortress for the 9th Legion. By AD 71 it had become a home for retired legionary soldiers. The town walls were first established in this period and some bits still remain, such as Newport Arch. Another landmark of the Roman era is the Fosse Dyke, dating from AD 120 it is the oldest canal in England.

Invasion from the east along Lincolnshire's coast then became the order of the day when the northern Germanic tribes, the Angles, Saxons and Jutes, paid a visit to British shores following Roman withdrawal. Over the next two centuries the Anglo-Saxon people, as we know them, expelled the native Britons pushing them back into Scotland and Wales eventually combining under Ecgberht in AD 802 to form the first English kingdom. Then along came the Danes in the 9th century. Their influence was widespread within the county and today the numerous towns and villages that end with '-by', '-wick' and '-toft' tell of their Viking origins.

Throughout medieval times the area flourished. Many large churches, abbeys and monasteries date from this period and Lincoln became a prosperous trading town. The magnificent Norman cathedral, built from the local limestone, dates from AD 1072, but most of the original structure collapsed during an earthquake and only very small sections of the west front and west towers survive from the original building, most of it dates from the 13th century. The cathedral is Gothic in style and is a spectacular sight as it presides over the city and the surrounding countryside. Its three towers can be seen sitting high above the city from miles around.

The Industrial Revolution, which had such a dramatic impact on many parts of the north of England and the midlands largely passed Lincolnshire by, which is partly why it is such a walkers' paradise today. However, the county played an important role during the Second World War when many airfields sprouted up. RAF Scampton was where the 617 'Dambusters' Squadron left for the bombing raids on the Ruhr dams. Squadron Leader Guy Gibson's dog was run over and killed the day before the raids and was buried here as he requested. Just down the road is RAF Coningsby, home to the Battle of Britain Memorial Flight aircraft. The Visitor Centre commemorates 'the Few' who safeguarded Britain against German invasion during late summer 1940. The flight comprises a Lancaster, five Spitfires, two Hurricanes, a couple of Chipmunks and a Douglas Dakota.

Fields southwest of Tealby Thorpe

Lincolnshire Wolds

The Wolds were designated as an Area of Outstanding Natural Beauty (AONB) in 1973. The title speaks for itself; this 47 mile (75km) long strip of rolling chalk and sandstone hills and secluded valleys is beautiful; a real rural idyll and walkers' paradise. The Wolds lie in the north-east of the county about half way between the city of Lincoln and the coast. There are some pretty towns and villages in the area. Alford, on the southeast edge of the Wolds is worth a visit as it has a superb five-sailed windmill. Just to the northwest is the 'capital of the Wolds', Louth; a lovely market town whose church, St James, has the highest medieval church steeple in England at 295ft (90m) tall. The town also has the distinction of being the most northerly town in the world that is sited on the Greenwich Prime Meridian. Just to the west of Louth are Hubbard's Hills where there is a spectacular steep sided valley about 130ft (40m) deep. This was cut about 20,000 years ago by glacial melt-water.

Walking tips & guidance

Safety

As with all other outdoor activities, walking is safe provided a few simple commonsense rules are followed:

- Make sure you are fit enough to complete the walk;

- Always try to let others know where you intend going, especially if you are walking alone;

- Be clothed adequately for the weather and always wear suitable footwear;

- Always allow plenty of time for the walk, especially if it is longer or harder than you have done before;

- Whatever the distance you plan to walk, always allow plenty of daylight hours unless you are absolutely certain of the route;

- If mist or bad weather come on unexpectedly, do not panic but instead try to remember the last certain feature which you have passed (road, farm, wood, etc.). Then work out your route from that point on the map but be sure of your route before continuing;

- Do not dislodge stones on the high edges: there may be climbers or other walkers on the lower crags and slopes;

- Unfortunately, accidents can happen even on the easiest of walks. If this should be the case and you need the help of others, make sure that the injured person is safe in a place where no further injury is likely to occur. For example, the injured person should not be left on a steep hillside or in danger from falling rocks. If you have a mobile phone and there is a signal, call for assistance. If, however, you are unable to contact help by mobile and you cannot leave anyone with the injured person, and even if they are conscious, try to leave a written note explaining their injuries and whatever you have done in the way of first aid treatment. Make sure you know exactly where you left them and then go to find assistance. Make your way to a telephone, dial 999 and ask for the police or mountain rescue. Unless the accident has happened within easy access of a road, it is the responsibility of the police to arrange evacuation. Always give accurate directions on how to find the casualty and, if possible, give an indication of the injuries involved;

- When walking in open country, learn to keep an eye on the immediate foreground while you admire the scenery or plan the route ahead. This may sound difficult but will enhance your walking experience;

- It's best to walk at a steady pace, always on the flat of the feet as this is less tiring. Try not to walk directly up or downhill. A zigzag route is a more comfortable way of negotiating a slope. Running directly downhill is a major cause of erosion on popular hillsides;

- When walking along a country road, walk on the right, facing the traffic. The exception to this rule is, when approaching a blind bend, the walker should cross over to the left and so have a clear view and also be seen in both directions;

- Finally, always park your car where it will not cause inconvenience to other road users or prevent a farmer from gaining access to his fields. Take any valuables with you or lock them out of sight in the car.

Equipment

Equipment, including clothing, footwear and rucksacks, is essentially a personal thing and depends on several factors, such as the type of activity planned, the time of year, and weather likely to be encountered.

All too often, a novice walker will spend money on a fashionable jacket but will skimp when it comes to buying footwear or a comfortable rucksack. Blistered and tired feet quickly remove all enjoyment from even the most exciting walk and a poorly balanced rucksack will soon feel as though you are carrying a ton of bricks. Well designed equipment is not only more comfortable but, being better made, it is longer lasting.

Clothing should be adequate for the day. In summer, remember to protect your head and neck, which are particularly vulnerable in a strong sun and use sun screen. Wear light woollen socks and lightweight boots or strong shoes. A spare pullover and waterproofs carried in the rucksack should, however, always be there in case you need them.

Winter wear is a much more serious affair. Remember that once the body starts to lose heat, it becomes much less efficient. Jeans are particularly unsuitable for winter wear and can sometimes even be downright dangerous.

Waterproof clothing is an area where it pays to buy the best you can afford. Make sure that the jacket is loose-fitting, windproof and has a generous hood. Waterproof overtrousers will not only offer complete protection in the rain but they are also windproof. Do not be misled by flimsy nylon 'showerproof' items. Remember, too, that garments made from rubberised or plastic material are heavy to carry and wear and they trap body condensation. Your rucksack should have wide, padded carrying straps for comfort.

It is important to wear boots that fit well or shoes with a good moulded sole – blisters can ruin any walk! Woollen socks are much more comfortable than any other fibre. Your clothes should be comfortable and not likely to catch on twigs and bushes.

It is important to carry a compass, preferably one of the 'Silva' type as well as this guide. A smaller scale map covering a wider area can add to the enjoyment of a walk. Binoculars are not essential but are very useful for spotting distant stiles and give added interest to viewpoints and wildlife. Although none of the walks in this guide venture too far from civilisation, on a hot day even the shortest of walks can lead to dehydration so a bottle of water is advisable.

Finally, a small first aid kit is an invaluable help in coping with cuts and other small injuries.

Public Rights of Way

In 1949, the National Parks and Access to the Countryside Act tidied up the law covering rights of way. Following public consultation, maps were drawn up by the Countryside Authorities of England and Wales to show all the rights of way. Copies of these maps are available for public inspection and are invaluable when trying to resolve doubts over little-used footpaths. Once on the map, the right of way is irrefutable.

Right of way means that anyone may walk freely on a defined footpath or ride a horse or pedal cycle along a public bridleway. No one may interfere with this right and the walker is within his rights if he removes any obstruction along the route, provided that he has not set out purposely with the intention of removing that obstruction. All obstructions should be reported to the local Highways Authority.

In England and Wales rights of way fall into three main categories:

• Public Footpaths – for walkers only;

• Bridleways – for passage on foot, horseback, or bicycle;

• Byways – for all the above and for motorized vehicles

Free access to footpaths and bridleways does mean that certain guidelines should be followed as a courtesy to those who live and work in the area. For example, you should only sit down to picnic where it does not interfere with other walkers or the landowner. All gates must be kept closed to prevent stock from straying and dogs must be kept under close control – usually this is interpreted as meaning that they should be kept on a leash. Motor vehicles must not be driven along a public footpath or bridleway without the landowner's consent.

Footpath west of Tealby Thorpe

Bridge on the Viking Way

A farmer can put a docile mature beef bull with a herd of cows or heifers, in a field crossed by a public footpath. Beef bulls such as Herefords (usually brown/red colour) are unlikely to be upset by passers by but dairy bulls, like the black and white Friesian, can be dangerous by nature. It is, therefore, illegal for a farmer to let a dairy bull roam loose in a field open to public access.

The Countryside and Rights of Way Act 2000 (the 'right to roam') allows access on foot to areas of legally defined 'open country' – mountain, moor, downland, heath and registered common land. You will find these areas shaded orange on the maps in this guide. It does not allow freedom to walk anywhere. It also increases protection for Sites of Special Scientific Interest, improves wildlife enforcement legislation and allows better management of Areas of Outstanding Natural Beauty.

The Country Code

The Country Code has been designed not as a set of hard and fast rules, although they do have the backing of the law, but as a statement of commonsense. The code is a gentle reminder of how to behave in the countryside. Walkers should walk with the intention of leaving the place exactly as it was before they arrived. There is a saying that a good walker 'leaves only footprints and takes only photographs', which really sums up the code perfectly.

Never walk more than two abreast on a footpath as you will erode more ground by causing an unnatural widening of paths. Also try to avoid the spread of trodden ground around a boggy area. Mud soon cleans off boots but plant life is slow to grow back once it has been worn away.

Have respect for everything in the countryside, be it those beautiful flowers found along the way or a farmer's gate which is difficult to close.

Stone walls were built at a time when labour costs were a fraction of those today and the special skills required to build or repair them have almost disappeared. Never climb over or onto stone walls; always use stiles and gates.

Dogs which chase sheep can cause them to lose their lambs and a farmer is within his rights if he shoots a dog which he believes is worrying his stock.

The moors and woodlands are often tinder dry in summer, so take care not to start a fire. A fire caused by something as simple as a discarded cigarette can burn for weeks, once it gets deep down into the underlying peat.

When walking across fields or enclosed land, make sure that you read the map carefully and avoid trespassing. As a rule, the line of a footpath or right of way, even when it is not clearly defined on the ground, can usually be followed by lining up stiles or gates.

Obviously flowers and plants encountered on a walk should not be taken but left for others passing to enjoy. To use the excuse 'I have only taken a few' is futile. If everyone only took a few the countryside would be devastated. If young wild animals are encountered they should be left well alone. For instance, if a fawn or a deer calf is discovered lying still in the grass it would be wrong to assume that it has been abandoned. Mothers hide their offspring while they go away to graze and browse and return to them at feeding time. If the animals are touched it could mean that they will be abandoned as the human scent might deter the mother from returning to her offspring. Similarly with baby birds, who have not yet mastered flight; they may appear to have been abandoned but often are being watched by their parents who might be waiting for a walker to pass on before coming out to give flight lesson two!

What appear to be harmful snakes should not be killed because firstly the 'snake' could be a slow worm, which looks like a snake but is really a harmless legless lizard, and second, even if it were an adder (they are quite common) it will escape if given the opportunity. Adders are part of the pattern of nature and should not be persecuted. They rarely bite unless they are handled; a foolish act, which is not uncommon; or trodden on, which is rare, as the snakes are usually basking in full view and are very quick to escape.

Map reading

Some people find map reading so easy that they can open a map and immediately relate it to the area of countryside in which they are standing. To others, a map is as unintelligible as ancient Greek! A map is an accurate but flat picture of the three-dimensional features of the countryside. Features such as roads, streams, woodland and buildings are relatively easy to identify, either from their shape or position. Heights, on the other hand, can be difficult to interpret from the single dimension of a map. The Ordnance Survey 1:25,000 mapping used in this guide shows the contours at 5 metre intervals. Summits and spot heights are also shown.

The best way to estimate the angle of a slope, as shown on any map, is to remember that if the contour lines come close together then the slope is steep – the closer together the contours the steeper the slope.

Learn the symbols for features shown on the map and, when starting out on a walk, line up the map with one or more features, which are recognisable both from the map and on the ground. In this way, the map will be correctly positioned relative to the terrain. It should then only be necessary to look from the map towards the footpath or objective of your walk and then make for it! This process is also useful for determining your position at any time during the walk.

Let's take the skill of map reading one stage further: sometimes there are no easily recognisable features nearby: there may be the odd clump of trees and a building or two but none of them can be related exactly to the map. This is a frequent occurrence but there is a simple answer to the problem and this is where the use of a compass comes in. Simply place the map on the ground, or other flat surface, with the compass held gently above the map. Turn the map until the edge is parallel to the line of the compass needle, which should point to the top of the map. Lay the compass on the map and adjust the position of both, making sure that the compass needle still points to the top of the map and is parallel to the edge. By this method, the map is orientated in a north-south alignment. To find your position on the map, look out for prominent features and draw imaginary lines from them down on to the map. Your position is where these lines cross. This method of map reading takes a little practice before you can become proficient but it is worth the effort.

Viking Way north of Belchford

How to use this book

This book contains route maps and descriptions for 20 walks, with areas of interest indicated by symbols (see below). For each walk particular points of interest are denoted by a number both in the text and on the map (where the number appears in a circle). In the text the route instructions are prefixed by a capital letter. We recommend that you read the whole description, including the fact box at the start of each walk, before setting out.

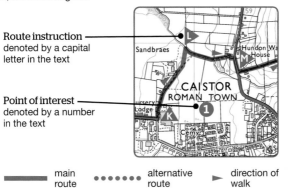

Route instruction denoted by a capital letter in the text

Point of interest denoted by a number in the text

──────── main route

•••••••• alternative route

▶ direction of walk

Key to walk symbols

At the start of each walk there is a series of symbols that indicate particular areas of interest associated with the route.

🐦 Birdlife   🐾 Other wildlife   ❀ Wild flowers

☀ Good views   🏰 Historical interest   🌳 Woodland

⛏ Geology   📖 Literature

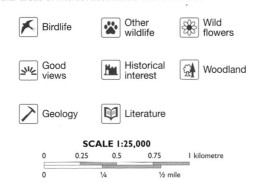

SCALE 1:25,000

| 0 | 0.25 | 0.5 | 0.75 | 1 kilometre |

| 0 | ¼ | ½ mile |

Please note the scale for walk maps is 1:25,000 unless otherwise stated
North is always at the top of the page

❝ A gentle stroll around the Gibraltar Point Nature Reserve, taking in some of the best viewpoints and hide locations **❞**

Whilst much of England's east coast is disappearing into the North Sea, at Gibraltar Point new land is being created all the time due to coastal deposition. A bracing walk around the reserve not only shows geography in action, there is also plenty of bird and plant life to have a look at too, and it's all explained with the aid of excellent interactive and audio-visual displays in the Visitor Centre.

A freshwater lagoon at
Gibraltar Point Nature Reserve

Gibraltar Point

Gibraltar Point
Nature Reserve

Plan your walk

Kingston upon Hull
Scunthorpe • Immingham
Grimsby
Louth
Lincoln
Skegness
Sleaford Boston
Grantham The
Wash
Spalding

DISTANCE: 2½ miles (4km)

TIME: 1¼ hours

START/END: TF556581
Park in Gibraltar Point
Visitor Centre car park

TERRAIN: Easy

MAPS:
OS Explorer 274;
OS Landranger 122

Route instructions

A Leave the car park at its northeastern end and follow the path which heads to the footbridge.

1 Gibraltar Point National Nature Reserve, which extends to over 1000 acres (430ha) situated here on the coast just south of Skegness, comprises a mixture of sandy and muddy shoreline as well as extensive sand-dunes, ponds, lagoons and both salt and fresh water marshes.

The reserve is an area of coastal deposition where material eroded by the action of the sea from the coast to the north has been transported south by a process called longshore drift. The western dunes

were originally right on the coast but are now about half a mile or so (1km) inland.

Birdlife to be seen at the reserve includes little terns, redshanks, lapwings and ringed plovers, all of which breed here, and during the autumn and winter months spectacular numbers of overwintering or migrating birds can be seen.

B After the second metal boundary post (marked with TTD), turn right opposite the Bean's Hole pond and information board. Follow the path keeping the sand dunes to your left.

C Upon reaching the Bird Observatory, turn left, with the Observatory to your

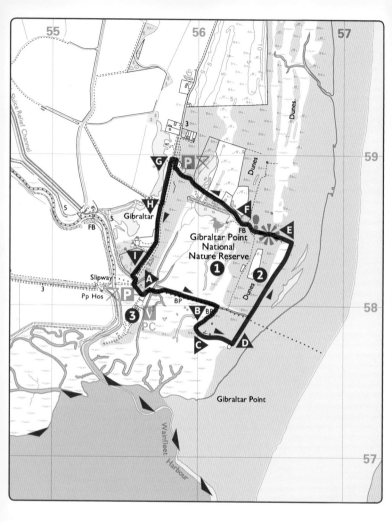

left. Follow the path past the viewpoint, keeping the dunes to your left.

D When you reach the Shorebird Warden's Base, go past it and then turn left. Look out for the wind turbines in the distance in front of you. Follow the

path heading towards the turbines keeping the dunes to your left.

2 Coastal sand dunes are a very fragile environment until they become stabilized by vegetation. The older dunes on the reserve have developed a fine turf where

Gibraltar Point

a variety of wildflowers can be found, a little like that of the chalk downland on the Wolds. Sea buckthorn is also widespread on the reserve and, in late summer and autumn, is covered in striking bright orange berries.

E At a crossroads in the path, turn left, heading inland over the dunes. Go up some steps towards a viewpoint and then down some steps the other side.

F Bear right and follow the main path past Fenland Lagoon East Hide. Continue on passing Mere Hide on your right until you reach a car park.

G Leave the car park at its northern end and cross the road into Croftmarsh Local Nature Reserve via a metal gate. Turn left onto the path and follow it as it runs southwest, parallel to the road, with a fence on the left.

H Pass through a gate, over a track and then continue along the path. Go past a path on your right to Jackson's Marsh Hide.

I Cross over a track signed to Syke's Farm Nature Reserve Office. The path then goes into a wooded area before joining a road. Turn right onto the road, over an embankment and back to the car park near the Visitor Centre.

3 The Visitor Centre located at the reserve has interactive displays, 3-D models and information on the wildlife and the environmental importance of the site.

Pond at Gibraltar Point Nature Reserve

" This walk takes you past the historic five-sailed working windmill at Alford and across the fields to the north with good views of the village and surrounding countryside "

The ancient market town of Alford lies on the southeast edge of the Wolds. There must have been a ford here in the past as the name means 'alder trees growing by the ford'. Nowadays, as is commonly the case, a bridge has replaced the ford. The town has a thriving local community and holds regular craft markets and auctions.

Alford

St Wilfrid's church

Route instructions

A Leave Millers Way car park via the entrance and turn left, then first left up Mill Close. Take the footpath ahead and slightly to the right of you signposted 'Bilsby'. Follow path turning right and then almost immediately left across a footbridge, continue up the left hand side of the field through a kissing gate. Cross the next field diagonally to the right.

B Go through hedge via two gates. Cross the next field bearing left to the kissing gate in the corner and follow path to the road. Turn left at the road and then right up the A1104. You will see Alford Windmill on your left. Carry on up the main road out of the village.

1 The superb five-sailed, seven-storey Alford Windmill dates from 1837, is still in use today and is open to visitors; you can buy a range of organic flours or taste the cooked version in the form of cakes and scones in the tea shop.

C Take the footpath on the right beyond the houses and follow the path with a hedge to your right. Cross footbridge and carry straight on up the field towards a tree on the horizon. Then bear left and head downhill to the corner of the field.

D Turn left on the lane and almost immediately right through a kissing gate, beside a hedge and then straight across a field.

Plan your walk

Kingston upon Hull
Scunthorpe • Immingham
Grimsby

Louth

• Lincoln

Skegness

Sleaford Boston
• Grantham The Wash

• Spalding

DISTANCE: 4¼ miles (6.75km)

TIME: 2¼ hours

START/END: TF457762 Park in the free car park on Millers Way

TERRAIN: Easy

MAPS:
OS Explorer 274;
OS Landranger 122

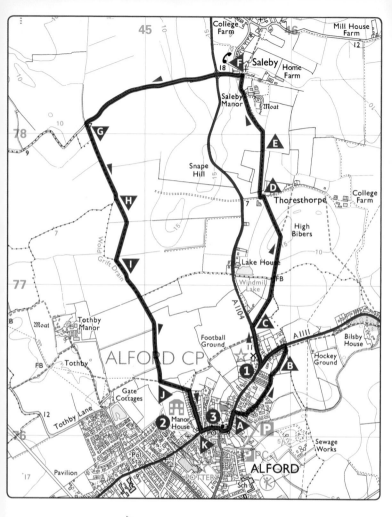

E Go over footbridge and follow the path with a hedge to your right. At post bear left aiming for the left hand corner of a farm building. Then follow track to the road.

F At the road turn left, cross the main road and continue on the lane opposite. The lane heads gently downhill. Follow road for ½ mile (1km).

G Opposite a hedgerow on the right, cross the footbridge on the left; you are now heading towards the village, look out for the windmill and church tower

Alford

on the horizon. Continue with a ditch on your right.

H When the ditch veers to the right, continue straight ahead across the field, cross a footbridge and bear right across the field heading to the right of a hedgerow at other side.

I Bear left over a footbridge and follow the field edge with a ditch on the right in the general direction of the church tower; cross another footbridge, again heading for the church. The path then curves to the right following the ditch.

J Cross the footbridge and stile and then bear left across a field, through a kissing gate, then bear right to the corner of the next field and onto Park Lane. Follow the road to the end and on the right you will see Alford Manor House.

2 The Grade II listed, brick-built, Alford Manor House dates from 1611 and is thought to be the largest thatched manor house in the country. At first glance you don't notice the thatch as the manor's appearance is so unlike most thatched buildings. It has quite an imposing frontage, more like a town house than the usual squat country cottage where the roof dominates.

K Turn left and follow the main road through the village, past the church on your left, back to the car park on the right.

3 St Wilfrid's church dates from about the 14th century and, in common with many buildings of this age, underwent some restoration during the Victorian era when the tower was altered and made more decorative.

Alford Manor House

> 66 This lovely city walk takes you alongside the River Witham for a short distance and then climbs up the aptly named Steep Hill towards Ellis Windmill and then past the castle to Lincoln Cathedral 99

The history of the city of Lincoln can be traced back about 2000 years when there was an Iron Age settlement here. The city is on a hill and due to its strategic position the Romans decided to build a fortress here in about AD 60, this became an important Roman administrative centre *(Lindum Colonia)*. However, as you approach the city the most striking structure you will see is the stunning Gothic cathedral sitting on top of the hill which is visible from miles around.

Waterside Shopping Centre on

Lincoln

Looking up Steep Hill

Route instructions

A From Silver Street car park turn left down Free School Lane. Turn left at St Swithin's Church and right into Thorngate, in front of you is the River Witham. Turn right and walk along the riverside passing a footbridge and the Millennium sculpture on the left. Climb up the steps to the High Street and turn right.

B Pass through Stonebow arch continuing north uphill, forking right into The Strait which becomes Steep Hill. Continue past bollards with high brick wall to your right. After passing the road Michaelgate on the left take the next left onto Wordsworth Street and continue straight on into Drury Lane.

C Turn right into Union Road, on the left is The Lawn.

1 Within the grounds of The Lawn is the Sir Joseph Banks Tropical Conservatory. It contains various plants from the species collected by Sir Joseph Banks who was botanist on Cook's voyage to Australia. About 80 species bear Banks' name. The Conservatory is also home to a massive Koi carp.

D At the end of Union Road turn left into Burton Road and left again onto a footpath immediately before Occupation Road. On the path turn right in front of two houses and continue on the path to Upper Long Leys Road where you turn

Plan your walk

Kingston upon Hull

Scunthorpe • Immingham
• Grimsby

• Louth

● Lincoln

• Skegness

• Sleaford Boston
• Grantham The Wash

• Spalding

DISTANCE: 2½ miles (4km)

TIME: 1¼ hours

START/END: SK977713 Silver Street Car Park, there are also car parks/ possible starting points at Grantham Street and Westgate Street

TERRAIN: Moderate; one steep hill

MAPS:
OS Explorer 272;
OS Landranger 121

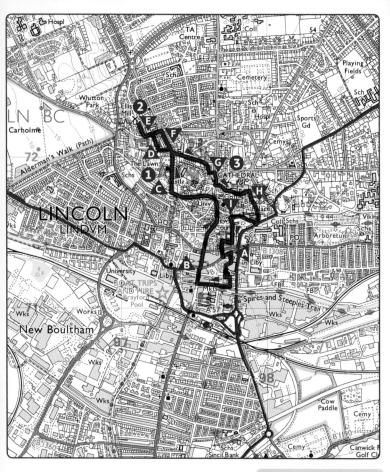

left and then right into Mill Road. Ellis Mill is about 100yds (100m) along this road on the left.

2 The lovely four-sailed Ellis Windmill dates from 1798 and was once one of nine windmills in this windy spot. Sadly, this is the only one left and you now come across it unexpectedly as it sits between rows of terraced houses. Having

been rescued from dereliction, the windmill, with its little white cap, was restored between 1977 and 1981; and it is still in full working order today and can be seen busy grinding flour on windy days.

E From the mill retrace your steps back along Mill Road and turn left into Upper Long Leys Road. The Museum of Lincolnshire Life

Lincoln

is the red brick crenellated building on your left.

F Turn right on Burton Road then left along Westgate at the mini roundabout. Turn right down St Pauls Lane, left into Gordon Road and right into Bailgate. Upon reaching the crossroads, Lincoln Castle is on your right.

G With the castle behind you pass through the arch towards the west front of the Cathedral and pass to its right hand side.

3 In its first few centuries Lincoln Cathedral had a bit of a chequered history: building began in 1072 and it was consecrated in 1092; it suffered from a fire in 1141 and then in 1185 the building was all but destroyed by an earthquake. A great deal of building work then took place in the 13th century and for almost 250 years the cathedral was reputably the tallest building in the world; but in 1549 the central spire, thought to be about 525 feet (158m) high, collapsed, never to be replaced. Most of the current building we see today dates from the 13th century, and extremely impressive it is too. It makes a spectacular sight as it presides over the city and the surrounding countryside. Its three towers can be seen sitting high above the city from miles around.

H At the eastern end of the Cathedral turn right down Greestone Place. This leads through an arch, down some steps and onto Lindum Road. Turn immediately right in front of the Greestone Centre (University of Lincoln) and up some steps on the right into Temple Gardens. Carry straight on with the remains of the Roman wall and Bishop's Old Palace on your right.

I Leave the gardens and turn left into Danesgate. Walk downhill then right into Grantham Street, left onto Flaxengate and cross over Clasketgate onto a short pedestrian section. Turn left into Silver Street and then turn right to the car park.

Lincoln Cathedral

On visiting the villages of Aby, Belleau and Claythorpe, our route comes across a churchyard without a church, a mediaeval mud dovecote and evidence of the old Lincolnshire mainline railway.

The village of Aby through which our walk passes, used to have a railway line and before its closure on 11th September 1961, the station had the distinction of having the shortest name on the British Rail network. You can see evidence of the railway's existence if you look for it: a goods shed near Claythorpe, a railway bridge and a pub called the Railway Tavern. The Great Eau river flows nearby, where you may see swallows swooping for flies during the summer months.

Aby & Claythorpe

Footpath to north of Aby

Route instructions

A From New Street, turn right along School Lane and just before the telephone box turn left onto the footpath between some houses. Go over a stile and then bear right across a field and head towards another stile. Cross the next field and turn right upon reaching the road.

B At the Railway Tavern take the footpath situated opposite and follow the path with the field boundary on your left-hand side. Go straight across a churchyard (which has no church) and upon emerging through a hedge bear left across the field to the signpost. Cross a footbridge and bear right following the field boundary.

1 The name of the Railway Tavern may seem a bit odd since there is no railway for miles around, but there used to be a station at Aby. It was a stop on the East Lincolnshire main line which ran from Grimsby to London. Here and there you can see the evidence of where the line used to run, but for the most part it has all but disappeared into the landscape.

C Cross the river via a footbridge and turn left to follow the path with the river to your left.

D Go through a gate by a cattle grid and turn right onto a track. Follow the track between some farm buildings and past an

Plan your walk

Kingston upon Hull
Scunthorpe · Immingham
· Grimsby

Louth

· Lincoln

Skegness

· Sleaford Boston
· Grantham The Wash

· Spalding

DISTANCE: 2½ miles (4km)

TIME: 1¼ hours

START/END: TF412783 Park safely in the village, for example on New Street

TERRAIN: Easy

MAPS: OS Explorer OL 283; OS Landranger 122

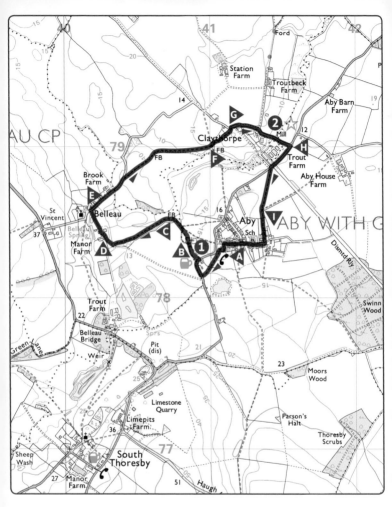

octagonal brick dovecote.
You have now reached the
village of Belleau.

E Upon reaching the road,
turn right and about 30yds
(30m) after passing the
Belleau village sign take
the footpath on your right.
Head across a field towards
a footbridge, cross this and
bear right with a stream to
your right, heading towards
a cottage.

F Pass to the left of the
cottage, turn right over
a stile and then bear left
following a track to the
road. You are now in the
hamlet of Claythorpe.

Aby & Claythorpe

G At the road turn right. The site of Aby station is on your right; the goods shed and station master's house can still be seen. Follow the road as it bends to the right, head downhill passing Claythorpe Mill on your right. Continue on the road to a 'T' junction.

2 Up until the 1970s what is now the Claythorpe Watermill & Wildfowl Gardens was a thriving watermill on the banks of the Great Eau river; grinding flour and also baking bread. Its demise was partly due to the closure, first by the local station at Aby in 1961, followed nine years later by the railway line itself. This resulted in the mill's route to market being cut off. These days it's open to visitors and there are over 300 birds, both familiar and more exotic, roaming in the pretty grounds. There is also information tracking the mill's history up until its closure. Take a break here and be sure to sample some of the homemade cakes in the tea room. Open daily from Easter until the end of September.

H Turn right and follow the road. Immediately after passing under a disused railway bridge take the footpath on the left. Head diagonally across the field.

I At the corner bear left to a stile. Follow the footpath until you eventually pass between two houses and through a wrought iron gate to reach the road. Turn right past the school building on the right and continue on back to the car.

Great Eau near Aby

A lovely walk past the lakes and through the parkland and open countryside around Culverthorpe Hall **99**

The village of Culverthorpe sits on the northern slopes of the Kesteven Uplands near the Lincolnshire Edge. The undulating landscape of this area, underlain by limestone, was moulded by a meltwater tributary of the River Trent just after the last ice age. This pretty walk, which passes by the large lake in front of Culverthorpe Hall, also passes close to the little village of Heydour with its lovely spired church.

Culverthorpe

View towards
Culverthorpe Park

Kingston upon Hull
Scunthorpe • Immingham
• Grimsby
• Louth
• Lincoln
Skegness
Sleaford Boston
• Grantham The Wash
• Spalding

DISTANCE: 3½ miles
(5.5km)

TIME: 1¾ hours

START/END: TF019399
Park in Culverthorpe
Walks car park to the
south of the lakes

TERRAIN: Easy

MAPS:
OS Explorer 248;
OS Landranger 130

Route instructions

A Leave the car park via the footpath in the northwest corner by an information board. Turn right onto the driveway with lakes on either side.

B At a bend in the drive turn right onto a path between railings. Views of the lake are to your right and Culverthorpe Hall to your left.

1 Set in some lovely parkland and presiding over a couple of lakes, Culverthorpe Hall, which is privately owned, was built from the local limestone around 1679 for Sir John Newton. It was the Newton family seat until 1761. There is a strange and rather sad story regarding the end of the Newton line: John Newton, Viscount Coningsby, the last male heir of the family and only a little baby at the time, was snatched from his cradle on 4th January 1733 by a pet monkey. The monkey scooted up to the roof of the hall along with his prize, with all and sundry in hot pursuit, whereupon the monkey dropped the baby over the parapet. Not surprisingly, the little viscount was killed.

C At a 'T' junction in the path turn left. Cross a stile and proceed, keeping the railings to your left. When you reach the driveway turn right. Walk through a small ornate metal gate to the left of a large one onto a road.

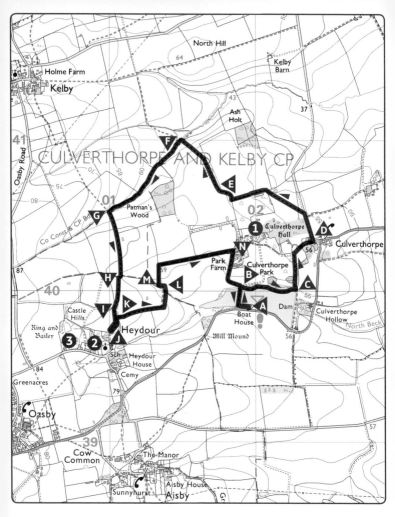

Continue for about 50yds (50m) to a junction.

D At the road junction, signed Kelby and Wilsford, turn left. Follow the lane for about 100yds (100m) and turn left onto a footpath. Bearing right go diagonally across a field, through a small woodland crossing two footbridges. Then turn left along the side of a field with a wood on your left.

E At a gap in the hedge turn right with the field boundary on your right. Go through a gap in the hedge and across a field

Culverthorpe

heading slightly to the left and downhill to a footbridge.

F Don't cross the footbridge but turn left in front of it, and follow the field boundary with the hedge to the right. Continue along the path, crossing a footbridge en route, Patman's Wood is on the hill to your left. Head for the corner of the field.

G Go through a gap in the hedge and turn left. Head uphill with the hedge to your left.

H Cross a bridleway and carry on straight ahead, over a footbridge and follow the path with the hedge to your left. The spire of Heydour church can be seen ahead.

I Follow the path and just after it bends to the right cross the footbridge to your left. Cross the road and over a stile, follow the path with the hedge to your left heading in direction of the church. (If you want to visit the church proceed straight ahead at this point and then retrace your steps to get back to the route.)

2 The lovely church of St Michael and All Angels in Heydour dates from Norman times although the elegant tower and spire were rebuilt in 1850. The church contains monuments to the Newton family, the first owners of Culverthorpe Hall.

3 To the west of the tiny village of Heydour is the site of a motte and bailey castle, which can be seen in the form of earthworks or 'lumps and bumps' and water-filled ditches on the current landscape. The castle appears to have been abandoned in the 14th century.

J Go over the stile and turn sharp left, and with the church behind you follow the path with the hedge to your left, heading northeast.

K Turn right across the track, over a stile and into a field. Continue straight ahead with a hedge to your left and the lake downhill to the right. Go over a stile into another field, follow field boundary round to the left, keeping the hedge to your left-hand side.

L Turn left at waymarked post.

M At next post ignore bridleway straight ahead and turn right with hedge to your left. Turn right at the corner of the field and with the hedge on your left head towards Park Farm.

N At a track turn right and follow it back to the car park.

St Michael's and All Angels church

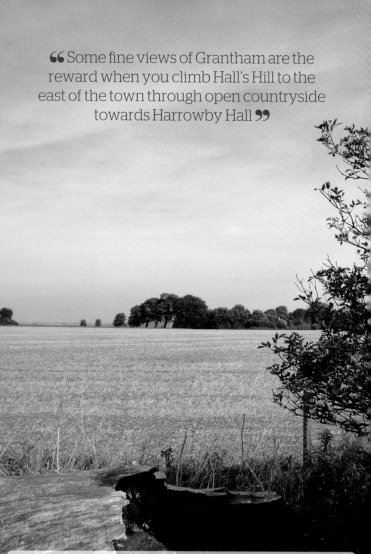

66 Some fine views of Grantham are the reward when you climb Hall's Hill to the east of the town through open countryside towards Harrowby Hall **99**

To the east of the market town of Grantham, probably best known as the birthplace of Margaret Thatcher, lies Hall's Hill from which you get some lovely views over the town and the surrounding countryside. Our walk takes us up the hill to Harrowby and then back down fairly steeply into the town again.

Grantham

View of Grantham

Route instructions

A Turn right out of the car park entrance and then left over the River Witham. Then turn left into the park with the river to your left.

B Turn right onto Stonebridge Road passing Grantham College on your left. At the cross roads go straight on into Beacon Lane. Continue on Beacon Lane uphill passing to the right of Avery Lodge Care Home.

C Just past Kenwick Drive (on your left) take the path on the left behind the houses and head for a small wooded area. Carry straight on and then turn left when you meet another path. Head downhill for a few yards.

D Ignoring the path which goes straight ahead into the housing estate, turn right. Follow this path with the hedge on your left. Go through a gap in the hedge and into a field. Continue round the left hand side of the field and gradually uphill.

E Carry straight on at end of the field ignoring the kissing gate to your right.

F At large copper beech tree and corner of field go straight on with the fence to your left, go past the entrance to Harrowby Hall on the right.

G At the Coach House bear right up Turnor Road. After about 550yds (500m), where the road bends

Plan your walk

Kingston upon Hull
Scunthorpe • Immingham
Grimsby
Louth
Lincoln
Skegness
Sleaford Boston
Grantham The Wash
Spalding

DISTANCE: 3¼ miles (5.25km)

TIME: 1¾ hours

START/END: SK917356 Park in Welham Street Pay and Display Car Park

TERRAIN: Moderate; some hills

MAPS:
OS Explorer 247;
OS Landranger 130

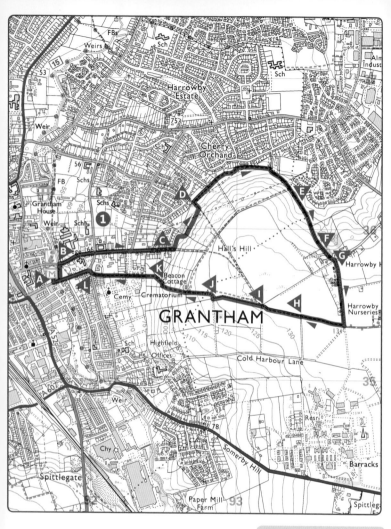

to the left, turn right onto a path that runs between hedges.

H▶ At a gap in the hedges go straight on through a field with a hedge to your right. There are good views of Grantham from here.

1 Grantham has the distinction of two extremely notable 'firsts' for women: it was where Britain's first woman Prime Minister, namely Margaret Thatcher, was born and went to school. She was PM from 1979 to 1990; it was also

Grantham

the first town to use female police officers when, in November 1914 during the First World War, Mary Allen and Ellen Harburn reported for duty.

Another of the town's luminaries is Sir Isaac Newton (1643–1727), the brilliant mathematician and physicist, who attended The King's Grammar School.

He is considered to be the most influential scientist of all time and the famous story regarding his inspiration – namely the apple falling to the ground from the tree due to the effects of gravity – is well known to all of us. His mother was keen for him to become a farmer and follow in his father's footsteps, at one time pulling him out of school. Luckily for all of us, he returned to finish his education.

▶ Where the path forks, take the left-hand path along the field boundary with a wood then a hedge to your right.

▶ Upon reaching a track, follow it to the right heading towards a house. Take the path to the left of the house, downhill and slightly to the right heading in the direction of a church spire. Continue along the path and through a scrubby bit of wood.

◖ Go through Grantham Cemetery, bear right and head for a kissing gate to the left of some houses. Continue down a path with the cemetery to your left, emerge onto a track, continue straight on until you reach a road.

◗ Cross over the road, bearing right onto St Catherine's Road, then turn left. Go down this road and turn left into Welham Street and the car park.

River Witham

66 Climbing to a height of 400ft (123m), this walk offers lovely views of the Wolds as it crosses open countryside to the south-west of the village of Binbrook **99**

The lovely little village of Binbrook nestled in the heart of the Lincolnshire Wolds only has a population of about 700 people but has a magnificent church seating 400, sometimes called the 'Cathedral of the Wolds'. The town was a small market town in the past with a larger population which may go some way to explain the size of the building.

Binbrook

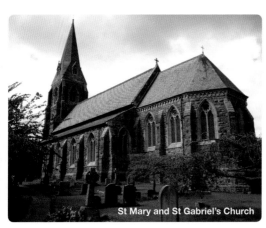

St Mary and St Gabriel's Church

Route instructions

A From Market Place, with the waterpump in the centre, head south in the direction of the road signposted 'Louth', passing Manor House and the Binbrook village sign on your left.

B Opposite The Plough, turn left and follow the road passing the church on the left and St Mary's Lane on the right.

1 There were originally two churches in the village sitting almost side by side: St Mary and St Gabriel. By the 1840s the former was in a poor state of repair and the latter was pretty much derelict. So it was decided to build one new church with a dual dedication on the site of St Mary's and

that's the superb late 19th century St Mary and St Gabriel's church building we see today.

C Just after Church View Business Centre take the bridleway to the right. Follow the track uphill and at the top, where there are good views over the village, church and surrounding countryside, turn right downhill along a footpath.

D At the bottom of the field go down some steps and across a small field, over a footbridge and stile and then pass between some houses to reach the road. Turn left and at the end of the road continue on the footpath keeping the hedge to your left. Go over

Plan your walk

Kingston upon Hull
Scunthorpe • Immingham
• Grimsby
• Louth
• Lincoln
Skegness
Sleaford Boston
• Grantham The Wash
• Spalding

DISTANCE: 3¼ miles (5km)

TIME: 1¾ hours

START/END: TF210939 Park in Market Place

TERRAIN: Moderate; some steep hills

MAPS:
OS Explorer 282;
OS Landranger 113

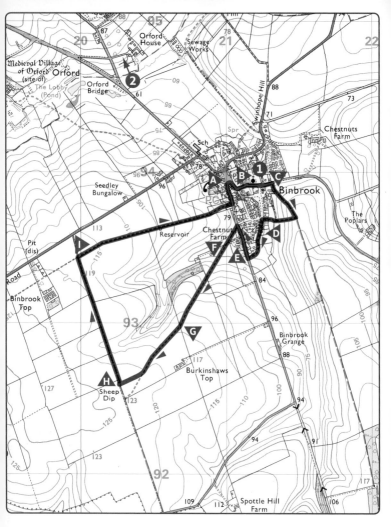

a stile and bear right across the field to another stile leading to Ludford Road.

E Turn right heading down then uphill for 220yds (200m). Near the top of the hill just before Ludford Road turns into High Street, turn left along a footpath between two hedges. At a stile bear right across a small field and go through a small gap in a wooden fence. Bear left across the corner of the field to a gap in the hedge.

Binbrook

F Carry on diagonally uphill across the field towards another gap in a hedge. Continue uphill across the next field in the general direction of a telegraph pole that can be seen on the horizon. Once near the top of the hill aim for a gap in the hedge at the far side of the field.

G Go through the gap in the hedge and head diagonally in a south-westerly direction across the next field; aim for a single ash tree and a gap in the hedge with a signpost.

H Turn right onto a bridleway. You are at the highest point of your walk here. There are good views towards Binbrook. Follow the bridleway with a hedge on your left until you reach a signpost.

I Turn right and keep the hedge to your right. You will see Binbrook church spire in front of you as you head towards the village. Follow the path gently downhill back to the village. On reaching High Street turn left and head back to the car.

❷ To the northwest of the village lies the disused Binbrook Airfield, opened in 1940 and home to RAF Binbrook until its closure in 1988. The base had close ties with the church of St Mary and St Gabriel. Inside the church there is a roll book listing those from the base who have fallen in action and a lovely stained-glass window is also testament to the close relationship between village and airbase.

The English Electric Lightning had its home here from 1962 until the base closed. This most iconic of fighters was designed and built in the UK and was the mainstay of Britain's air defence during the Cold War. Since the closure of the base the throb of these superb aircrafts' Rolls Royce Avon engines can no longer he heard at the site and nature is now reclaiming the runway.

Countryside south of Binbrook

66 A gentle stroll which takes you through the village of Branston and to the south and west of Branston Park where you are treated to glimpses of the impressive late 19th-century Hall sitting in its attractive parkland 99

The village of Branston which is situated only about 3 miles (5km) to the southeast of the city of Lincoln is dominated on its southwestern side by the large parkland of Branston Hall. Our walk takes us through part of the village and around the edge of the pretty 88 acre (35.5ha) grounds of the Hall, which is now a luxury hotel.

Branston

Countryside near Branston Hall

Plan your walk

Kingston upon Hull
Scunthorpe • Immingham
Grimsby
Louth
Lincoln
Skegness
Sleaford Boston
Grantham The
Wash
Spalding

DISTANCE: 2¼ miles (3.75km)

TIME: 1¼ hours

START/END: TF017676 Park in lay-by or village hall car park opposite Branston Hall

TERRAIN: Easy

MAPS:
OS Explorer 272;
OS Landranger 121

Route instructions

A From the lay-by or car park turn left into the village, past the water pump turning right in front of the Waggon and Horses pub.

B Immediately past the Waggon and Horses turn left up Church Hill past All Saints church. Keeping left you will see a car park in front of you, go through the car park and then take the footpath which runs to the right of the church hall.

1 All Saints church in Branston is an impressive building in Gothic style with its spire towering over the surrounding buildings. The earliest parts of the building date from Saxon times, but very little remains and much of the current building

is much more recent. Extensive restorations and extensions took place during Victorian times including work supervised by the renowned architect Sir George Gilbert Scott in 1875–76. Sir George is most famous for the superb Midland Grand Hotel at St Pancras station in London and is buried in Westminster Abbey.

There was a catastrophic fire in the church on Christmas Day 1962, following which quite a bit of restoration work needed to be done. The roof, organ, rood screen, chancel and east windows were lost. The replacement of the old east window with a brand new stained-glass window

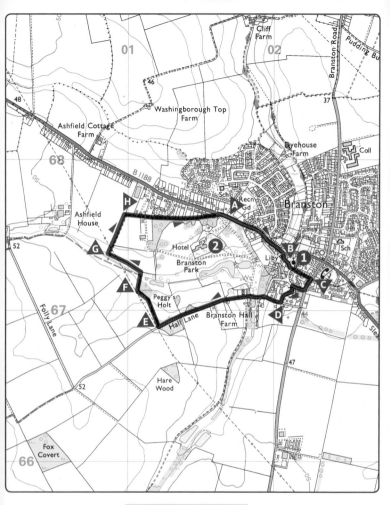

has not been universally popular as it looks a little at odds with the rest of the building, but, along with the lovely tapestry hassocks, it certainly provides a bright splash of colour as the light streams in.

C At the road turn right and then right again into

Chapel Road. Turn left in front of an attractive converted chapel into Chapel Lane.

D At the end of Chapel Lane turn right into Thackers Lane. Head downhill and on the left you will see Waterwheel Lane. You can take a short

Branston

diversion here if desired. If you turn left up Waterwheel Lane and follow it for about 220yds (200m) you will find a small disused waterwheel. Retrace your steps to rejoin the route. There is a sculpture where the stream meets the road. As you continue along the road, there is a slight climb.

E After passing through a small wood turn right onto a byway with a hedge on the right-hand side. On your right you may see glimpses of Branston Hall as you walk along.

2 Branston Hall, now a luxury hotel, is a typically imposing Victorian country house set in 88 acres (35.5ha) of lovely parkland with mature trees and a lake. It was built between 1884 and 1886 for the Melville family and has an impressive set of chimneys.

During World War II, as was the case with many country houses, it was commandeered for the war effort and was used as an RAF hospital.

F After a short while the path bends to the right with woodland to the right and crosses a small stream with stepping stones. Turn left with the hedge on the right and the stream on the left.

G Turn right when the hedge ends and follow the footpath with the hedge to your right along the edge of the field. Look out for a distant view of Lincoln Cathedral to your left.

H Two thirds of the way along the field turn right and follow the path, which runs behind some houses, back to the road. Turn right and head back to the car.

Branston Hall

> 66 Following the distinctive yellow and black Viking Way markers for about a third of the walk, our route starts in Caistor and takes us across attractive open countryside by way of the little village of Nettleton 99

The historic market town of Caistor through which our walk passes via part of the long distance 'Viking Way' footpath, is bursting at the seams with Grade II listed buildings. Although most of the town is Georgian, there are bits of it that are Roman such as a small fragment of wall to the south of the parish church of St Peter and St Paul. In 1793, Caistor was due to get its own canal in order to transport the local farm produce to the west of the county. In the end it never reached Caistor but Navigation Lane, which follows the intended route of the canal, can be seen to the west of the town.

Caistor

Countryside west of Caistor

Route instructions

A Turn left along North Street, take the footpath between walls on the left soon after Waterhills Court on the right. Follow this to the High Street.

1 Caistor, which sits in the lovely countryside on the northwestern edge of the Lincolnshire Wolds, comes from the Anglo-Saxon name *'ceaster'* which means Roman camp or town. Although the town has small remnants of its Roman origins, it mainly dates from Georgian times and has some fine buildings from this era. It is a real gem of a town.

B Turn left and then right into Market Place. Bear right down Plough Hill

which becomes Horse Market. The road bends to the right and becomes Nettleton Road.

C On the left you will see Redhills Close. Take the Viking Way footpath on the left immediately after it. Carry on into Westwold Road. Turn left at the end of the road and left again onto a footpath which runs behind the houses and up to the bypass.

D Carefully cross the bypass to the path opposite and down a steep path through a kissing gate. Follow the path with mature hedge to your left.

E Turn left over a footbridge and then through a gate.

Plan your walk

Kingston upon Hull
Scunthorpe • Immingham
• Grimsby
• Louth
• Lincoln
• Skegness
• Sleaford Boston
• Grantham The Wash
• Spalding

DISTANCE: 4 miles (6.25km)

TIME: 2 hours

START/END: TA118014 Park in the car park on North Street

TERRAIN: Moderate; some steep hills

MAPS:
OS Explorer 284;
OS Landranger 113

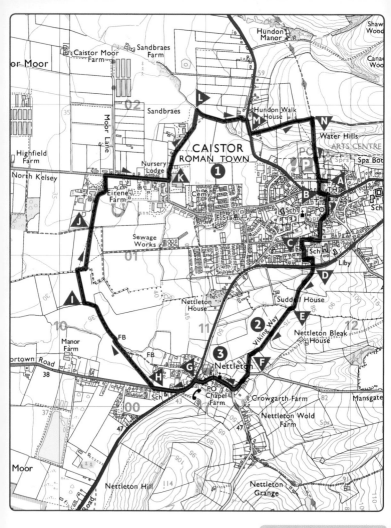

Carry straight on with hedge to right, pass through three kissing gates keeping the field boundaries to your right.

2 The Viking Way long distance footpath runs for 147 miles (237km) from the Humber Bridge all the way south to Oakham in Rutland. Our walk follows it for about 1¼ miles (2km). The route waymarks use the logo of a black Viking helmet on a bright yellow background. The route was established in 1976 by the Ramblers to highlight the

Caistor

influence of the Danelaw from about the 9th century when the Norsemen held sway in the county.

F Bear left keeping to the left of the buildings and continue onto a road and turn right into Nettleton village. At road junction turn right past the church.

3 St John the Baptist church in Nettleton mainly dates from 1874 and has a much older, rather crumbly, Saxon tower. The church clock, dating from 1837, was made by the nephew of John Harrison, the inventor of the marine chronometer.

G At the Salutation Inn cross the main road and turn left, then take the next road (Moortown Road) on the right.

H After Wood Farm Close, take the footpath on the right, go through a kissing gate and head diagonally across the field to the left of a brick building. Continue with a stream on the right. Cross the stream via a footbridge and then bear left passing through a kissing gate and follow the path.

I Turn right through a gate just before a Scots Pine. Follow the path keeping the hedge on your right. Cross a stream which

has been piped under the path and turn right. Almost immediately turn left at the post crossing the field to the other side.

J At signpost continue straight over footbridge and follow path to road and turn right.

K Where the road bends, turn left onto Sandbraes Lane and follow it. Turn right onto a footpath just past a house on the left.

L Go through a gate, down some steps, cross a footbridge, up some steps, through a kissing gate and turn right. Follow path with hedge to your right. Continue along the path going through a metal and then a wooden gate until you reach a road where you turn right.

M After about 110yds (100m) turn left onto a track (Canada Lane). Follow this up a steep hill passing Hundon Walk House on the left, continue on until you reach a four-way signpost.

N Turn right through a kissing gate, proceed downhill, across a stream and then up the other side of the valley. Go past cottages on the left and turn left onto North Street back to the car park.

Viking Way waymark

66 Taking in the lovely market town of Louth, our route passes in front of the superb 15th-century St James' church, and then heads up the impressive valley of Hubbard's Hills and into the open countryside beyond 99

Sitting on the eastern edge of the Lincolnshire Wolds, the town of Louth is presided over by the 15th-century church of St James which has the tallest spire of any English medieval church. Our route gives us a good look at the church as we pass next to it and then heads west to Hubbard's Hills to follow a spectacular 130ft (40m) deep gorge. Originally cut by glacial meltwater, the flat-bottomed valley now contains the gently meandering little River Lud which is much too small to have cut such a deep valley.

Louth & Hubbard's Hills

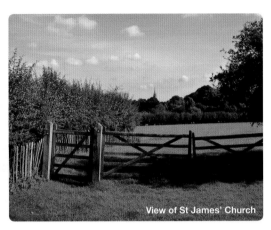

View of St James' Church

Route instructions

A Leave the car park and turn left following the path with the River Lud on your right. Turn right over footbridge and then left onto the road.

B After a few yards take the footpath on the left into Westgate Fields, follow this to the northeast entrance gate.

1 The lovely market town of Louth is known as the 'capital of the Lincolnshire Wolds' and sits on their eastern edge. The town takes its name from the River Lud on which it stands, whose name is derived from the Old English *'Hlude'* meaning 'noisy stream' or 'loud one'. Louth has the distinction of being the most

northerly town in the world that is sited on the Greenwich Meridian. One of the town's famous sons was the Victorian poet Alfred, Lord Tennyson, who went to Louth Grammar School.

C Leave the park and with a brick wall in front of you and a row of houses to the right, turn right onto Westgate heading into the town. At a fork in the road turn left and head towards the church.

2 The church of St James in Louth has the highest medieval church steeple in England rising to 295ft (90m). Built in the 15th century it is a magnificent building. The church was the site of the Lincolnshire Rising which led to the

Plan your walk

Kingston upon Hull
Scunthorpe · Immingham
Grimsby
Louth
· Lincoln
Skegness
· Sleaford Boston
· Grantham The Wash
· Spalding

DISTANCE: 4¼ miles (6.75km)

TIME: 2½ hours

START/END: TF315867
Park in the pay and display car park at Hubbard's Hills (note out of season restricted opening times)

TERRAIN: Moderate; with some gentle climbs

MAPS:
OS Explorer 283;
OS Landranger 122

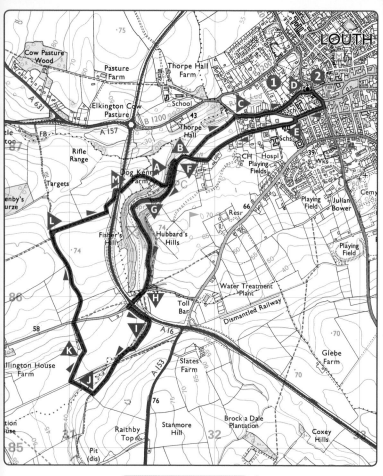

Pilgrimage of Grace in 1536. Getting involved in the Rising had dire repercussions for St James whose vicar was hanged at Tyburn and the church treasures, along with the rood screen, were plundered.

D Turn right in front of the church and then turn right again along Upgate. Then turn right down Gospelgate.

E At the end of Gospelgate turn left and then immediately right onto Crowtree Lane. Pass Irish Hill and Love Lane on the right and continue as the road runs beside Westgate Fields.

F Keep to the left hand side of the road taking the high path on top of the bank. Keep to the left of the railings and continue

Louth & Hubbard's Hills

climbing up through a beech wood. At a fork in the path take the right hand path downhill keeping the railings to your right.

G Emerge from the woods into an open area. Head down to the river on your right, across a footbridge, turn left with the river on your left. Cross a second footbridge and continue up the valley, through a gate into a small car park.

H Turn right on the road and go under the flyover and then immediately left onto a footpath. Follow the edge of the field with the hedge to your left.

I Go through a gap in the hedge and turn right following the field with the hedge to your right. Enter woodland and following the path, head up some steps onto an embankment, cross into the field opposite and turn right keeping the hedge to your right.

J Turn right through a gate onto a bridleway, cross a footbridge between two lakes and go through another gate. Cross a field, go through a gap in the hedge and up and over a disused railway. Bear right across a field.

K Cross a footbridge and bear left heading to the right of the cottages. Upon reaching the road take the bridleway opposite and bear diagonally right across the field. Go through a gate and follow the left-hand side of the field.

L At the corner of the field turn right onto a footpath with the hedge to your left. Follow the path and cross the main road with care.

M Cross stile and bear left. St James' church spire is ahead. Follow the left hand side of the field, over a stile and carry straight on to a gate. Then bear right across the field to the car park.

St James' Church

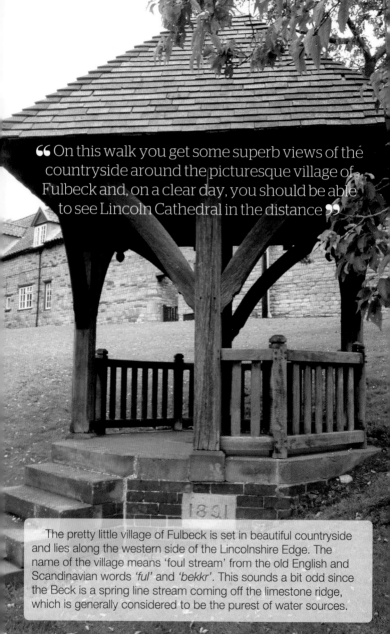

> **On this walk you get some superb views of the countryside around the picturesque village of Fulbeck and, on a clear day, you should be able to see Lincoln Cathedral in the distance**

1851

The pretty little village of Fulbeck is set in beautiful countryside and lies along the western side of the Lincolnshire Edge. The name of the village means 'foul stream' from the old English and Scandinavian words *'ful'* and *'bekkr'*. This sounds a bit odd since the Beck is a spring line stream coming off the limestone ridge, which is generally considered to be the purest of water sources.

Village pump, High Street

Fulbeck

St Nicholas' Church

Route instructions

A From the car park cross the main road and turn left. Turn right down Rectory Lane and then left down the High Street. Continue downhill ignoring the road Scott's Hill on the right.

B At the crossroads go straight on into Sudthorpe Hill and head, initially down then uphill. At the end of the road take the footpath between houses to the right of Fulbeck Cottage. Bear right across the field to a waymark post at the field boundary.

C At a gap in the hedge, cross the footbridge, turn left and continue with the hedge to your left.

D At the corner of the field turn right onto a track and continue for about 440yds (400m). Where the track bends to the right continue straight ahead. There are good views to both sides and Caythorpe church is visible to your left.

E Continue straight ahead on the bridleway at the junction where a footpath goes left. Carry on past a mast on the right, keeping the hedge to your left.

F Near the top of the hill turn right at the signpost and head downhill along the left-hand side of the field until you get to Reeve's Gorse woodland, where you turn right. After a short distance turn left through a gap in the hedge and continue down the

Plan your walk

Kingston upon Hull
Scunthorpe • Immingham
Grimsby
Louth
• Lincoln
Skegness
• Sleaford Boston
• Grantham The Wash
• Spalding

DISTANCE: 4¼ miles (6.75km)

TIME: 2½ hours

START/END: SK949504 Park in the car park opposite the churchyard

TERRAIN: Moderate; some hills

MAPS:
OS Explorer 272;
OS Landranger 121

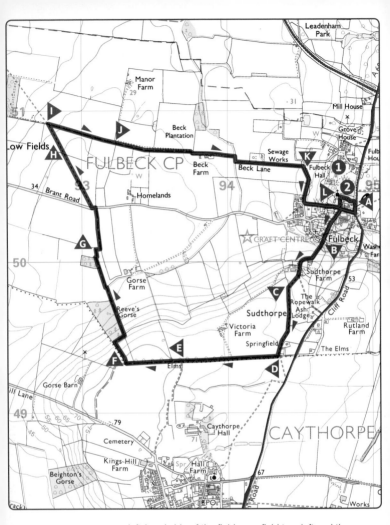

left-hand side of the field. Continue straight on through a gate keeping the hedge to your left.

G Where the hedgerow ends turn right to the other side of the field and then left with the hedge to your right. At the corner of the

field turn left and then go through a gate onto the road. Cross the road and take the footpath opposite. Bear left over the field.

H Cross the footbridge which is in a gap in the hedgerow, then bear left over the next field towards

Fulbeck

the corner roughly in the direction of Brant Broughton church spire.

▶ Go through a gap in the hedge and at the signpost turn right onto a bridleway, continue with the hedge on your right. You should see Fulbeck church tower ahead of you and on a good day Lincoln Cathedral on the horizon to the left.

▶ Pass through a gap in the hedge to the next field and continue straight ahead on the track. This eventually becomes a road, follow this past Beck Farm on the right back towards Fulbeck. On the hill ahead of you is Fulbeck Hall.

❶ Fulbeck Hall, located in the northern half of the village, has been the family seat of the Fane's for nearly four centuries. The building we see today dates from 1733 as the original structure was destroyed by fire. As with many stately homes, in 1943 the Hall was commandeered for the war effort. It became the headquarters for the 1st Airborne Division where it was witness to the planning of the battle of Arnhem in 1944. The Hall houses the Arnhem Museum which commemorates this event.

▶ At the 'T' junction turn right and then at the cross roads turn left into Rectory Lane and head uphill.

▶ Turn left in front of the Hare and Hounds pub, go through a gate into the churchyard and turn right towards the lychgate and cross the road to the car park.

❷ The oldest existing sections of the pretty church of St Nicholas in the village of Fulbeck date from Norman times, however, very little remains from this time and most of the current building is 13th to 15th century. Inside there are monuments to various members of the Fane family of Fulbeck Hall.

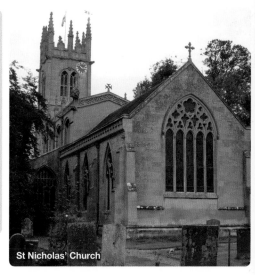

St Nicholas' Church

66 Denton reservoir, around which our route takes us, is a haven for birdlife; you should see plenty of ducks, coots and moorhens and even the beautiful great crested grebe if you are lucky 99

Taking in the pretty villages of Harlaxton and Denton, just to the south-west of Grantham, this lovely walk through open countryside heads north to touch on the Grantham Canal. Built in 1797 the canal closed in 1930 and fell into a state of serious disrepair. However, since 1969 a group of enthusiastic volunteers has been busy working on its restoration. It is a long slow process, but the canal is gradually being reclaimed and is a haven for all sorts of wildlife as well as a lovely area to walk. In July 2010 the wharf at Harlaxton was reopened. You can take a short detour at point ⓒ to have a look.

Harlaxton & Denton

Harlaxton village

Route instructions

A From the lay-by on the A607 head north up Peashill Lane.

B Where the track divides take the right hand fork, continue north with the hedge to your left.

C Cross the stile, (the Grantham Canal is in front of you), turn left onto a footpath and go over another stile. Cross the field to the far corner.

D Go over stile and footbridge. Carry straight on with the hedge to your left. Go through some small woodland, over a footbridge and up some steps to Denton reservoir. Turn right and follow the path around the reservoir.

1 The teardrop-shaped Denton Reservoir was created as a water supply for the Grantham Canal. It is replenished by small streams which flow from the hills to the south of Denton. Plenty of waterfowl make their home here including coots, moorhens and the great crested grebe.

E At southern end of reservoir carry straight on with the stream to your left.

F After a short while you cross a track (formerly a railway line) with stiles either side and continue along the path across the next field with the stream to your left. Cross a stile and continue on the path to a road, turn left into the village of Denton.

Plan your walk

Kingston upon Hull
Scunthorpe • Immingham
• Grimsby
Louth
• Lincoln
Skegness
Sleaford Boston
Grantham The Wash
Spalding

DISTANCE: 4¼ miles (6.75km)

TIME: 2½ hours

START/END: SK879327 Park in lay-by on the A607 at the junction with Peashill Lane

TERRAIN: Easy

MAPS: OS Explorer 247; OS Landranger 130

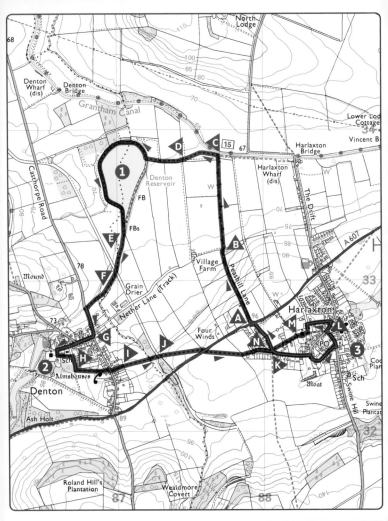

2 The picturesque village of Denton has a host of listed buildings, many built from the local golden ironstone. This small settlement is dominated to the west by the grounds of Denton Manor of which only the gatehouse remains.

Denton's attractive church of St Andrew primarily dates from the 14th to 16th centuries.

G In Denton turn right at the junction into Church Street. At the next junction keep left (signed 'Village

Harlaxton & Denton

only') and go past the 'Welby Arms'. Turn left in front of St Andrew's church then left again through a kissing gate and across a field with a wall on your left. Turn right onto the road.

H At the end of the road turn left behind Park Cottage, through a kissing gate and across a field to a footbridge. Continue between hedges to the road. Cross over the road and slightly to the right take the path between Orchard House and Briary House.

I Go over a stile and bear slightly right across a field. Go across a footbridge and head towards a stile at the edge of the field. Cross over the track of the disused railway and, opposite and slightly to the right, go through a squeeze gate.

J Bear right uphill across a field to its corner next to the A607. Carefully cross to the path on the other side. Bear left across the field and take the path to the left of a house via a stile. You are now entering the village of Harlaxton. Then go through a kissing gate onto West End (road).

3 The village of Harlaxton has a wealth of listed buildings including the lovely spired church of St Peter and St Mary, the earliest parts of which date from the 12th century. The village has an impressive manor house and park. It is located to the east of the village and is home to the British campus of the University of Evansville, USA. The lucky students are able to live and study in this huge Victorian manor, built in 1937, which sits at the end of a long straight drive. It is an impressive site with its mix of Gothic, Jacobean and Baroque styles.

K At the junction turn right onto Rectory Lane. Turn right into Pond Street then at the 'T' junction turn left onto High Street.

L At the obelisk turn right. Follow the road and turn first left up Trotters Lane and left again at the end into the churchyard. Follow the path around the church and exit the churchyard to the west.

M Go over a stile and turn left across a field with the hedge to your left. Go through a kissing gate passing in front of a brick building and then go through a gate. Cross the field diagonally bearing slightly left.

N Go through a kissing gate and turn right onto the road and follow this back to the lay-by.

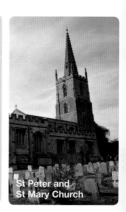
St Peter and St Mary Church

66 Starting and ending near Ayscoughfee Hall and Gardens this walk takes you along the Coronation Channel and then alongside the attractive tree-lined River Welland

The Georgian market town of Spalding, in the South Holland area of Lincolnshire, is probably best known as the bulb capital of Britain with the surrounding Fens area supplying over half of the flower bulbs grown in Britain. In the spring the annual flower parade with its superb floral floats attracts over 100,000 visitors to the town.

Spalding

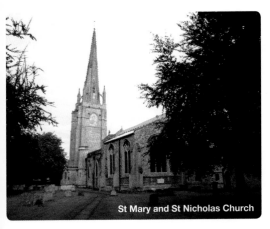

St Mary and St Nicholas Church

Route instructions

A Walk down The Vista towards the church of St Mary and St Nicholas passing through the churchyard to the left of the church. Go through the gate into Church Street and turn right. Follow the road round to the left.

B Turn right into Stonegate which is signposted 'Cowbit'. Continue along the road and go past the school which is to your left.

C Take the next road on the left (Matmore Gate). Go past 'South Holland Post 16 Centre' on your left and heading straight on take the bridleway over the bridge that crosses Coronation Channel.

1 The Coronation Channel, with its high embankments, was built in 1953 to try and alleviate the flooding that had taken place in Spalding on a frequent basis over the millennia. This allowed large areas of land to be built upon which were previously considered unsuitable. The channel runs to the east of the River Welland and is a haven for wildlife – you should see plenty of ducks and coots as you walk along the bank.

D Turn right onto the path which runs along the left-hand side of the channel. On the left is Arnold's Meadow Nature Reserve. Continue south crossing a narrow road and follow the bend in the channel to the right.

Plan your walk

Kingston upon Hull

Scunthorpe • Immingham

• Grimsby

Louth

• Lincoln

Skegness

• Sleaford Boston

• Grantham The Wash

Spalding

DISTANCE: 2¾ miles (4.25km)

TIME: 1½ hours

START/END: TF249224 Park in the lay-by at side of the road on Church Gate or in the Pay and Display car park off The Vista

TERRAIN: Easy

MAPS:
OS Explorer 249;
OS Landranger 131

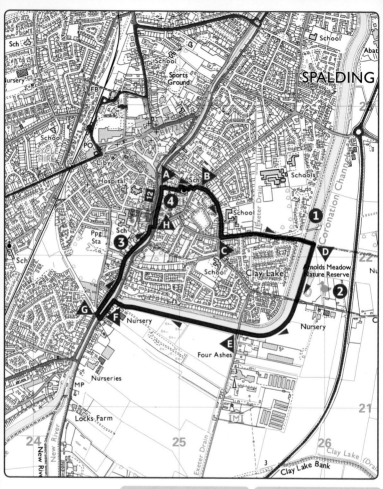

2 Before coming into the care of the Lincolnshire Wildlife Trust in 1968 Arnold's Meadow Nature Reserve area was just a plain ordinary field; now it is an ecologically diverse wildlife haven. A large part of the reserve's 6.5 acre (2.6ha) area is comprised of a traditionally managed hay meadow which is allowed to flood during the autumn and winter. There are also hedgerows, a small wood and open water areas. This variety of habitats encourages a wide range of flora and fauna. The reserve is home to water voles, kingfishers, grass snakes and at least seventeen species of butterfly have been spotted.

Spalding

E Cross another road then follow the channel until it reaches a gate.

F Go through the gate and you will see the River Welland in front of you. Turn left then right over the river via the footbridge beside the old disused railway bridge.

G Upon reaching the other side of the river turn right and walk north towards the centre of the town with the river to your right. Go past the first footbridge and take the second footbridge over the river at the point where Love Lane joins the main road on the eastern side.

3 The market town of Spalding lies on the River Welland and has been in existence since at least the 6th century. The town sits in an area of reclaimed marshland and estuary and the highly fertile silty soil has resulted in it becoming a major centre for flower and vegetable growing. The town is also one of the homes of the tasty sagey Lincolnshire sausage.

H Turn left, heading north with the river to your left. On your right is the brick wall of the Ayscoughfee Gardens. Follow this until you reach the museum building. It is worth having a look around the gardens which are very attractive and are free to enter, as is the museum. After leaving Ayscoughfee Hall turn right to return to your car.

4 Ayscoughfee Hall, which sits beside the River Welland as it flows through Spalding town centre, is housed in a Grade II* medieval country house dating back to around 1451. This superb building, entrance to which is free, has an ornate Gothic frontage and houses various exhibitions and displays including a gallery showing the changes to the South Holland area as a result of land drainage and reclamation. The museum is set in 5 acres (2ha) of attractive gardens which includes a war memorial designed by Edwin Lutyens.

Ayscoughfee Hall

> 66 This lovely walk through open countryside to the north of Belchford offers some extensive views over the Wolds. As you head north, on a clear day, you can see the World War II Chain Home radar mast, one of the few left in the country 99

Nestled amongst hills and valleys in the heart of the Lincolnshire Wolds about 5 miles (8km) to the north of Horncastle lies the little village of Belchford. The village is the venue for the Belchford Downhill Challenge which takes place every year in the middle of September on Furlong Lane, on the southeastern approach to the village. This exciting annual event brings competitors from far and wide in their exotic array of soapbox gravity carts. The carts pick up quite a speed on the hill and the course involves some tricky chicanes (using traffic cones) on which many of the competitors come unstuck.

Countryside between Belchford and Scamblesby looking north

Belchford

St Peter and St Paul church

Route instructions

A From the church, turn left and follow 'Main Road' out of the village to the west.

1 Although the current little church of St Peter and St Paul in Belchford is fairly new, dating from around the 19th century, a 16th century rector from the village, Nicholas Leache, was one of the ringleaders in the 1536 Lincolnshire Rising. Leache met a nasty end as a result of his activities when he was arrested and taken to Tyburn where he was hanged, drawn and quartered for treason.

B After about 880yds (800m), at a right hand bend in the road turn right up the bridleway through a white-painted gate between hedges. Follow the track gently uphill.

C After about ½ mile (1km) you pass Wood Farm (converted to holiday cottages) on your right. Ignore the driveway which heads off to the left and go through the gate which is ahead of you and then walk straight on along the bridleway with the hedge to your left. You are on the crest of the hill here with lovely views all around. The Chain Home mast is ahead of you and a modern transmitter to the left of it. Continue straight ahead to another gate.

2 To be seen in the distance to the north of our walk is the 350ft (106.5m) steel

Plan your walk

Kingston upon Hull
Scunthorpe · Immingham
Grimsby
Louth
· Lincoln
Skegness
· Sleaford Boston
· Grantham The Wash
· Spalding

DISTANCE: 4½ miles (7.25km)

TIME: 2¾ hours

START/END: TF294754
Park in lay-by just outside the church

TERRAIN: Moderate; some hills

MAPS:
OS Explorer 273;
OS Landranger 122

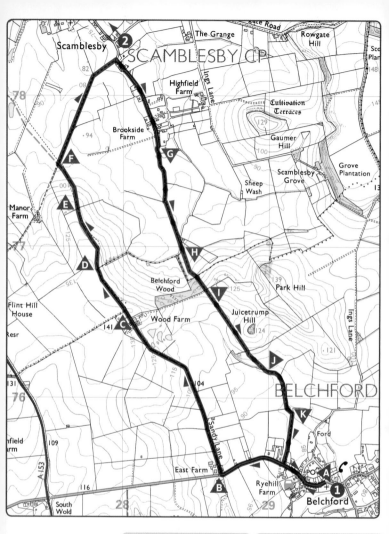

transmitter mast of RAF Stenigot, which was built in 1940 during World War II. It was part of the long range early-warning radar system, named 'Chain Home', one of a chain of radars along the eastern and southern coasts of Britain built in order to forewarn the RAF of Luftwaffe attacks.

D Go through the gate and across the field in the general direction of the Chain Home mast. Part way across this field at the brow of the hill, you should

Belchford

be able to see a water trough, head slightly to the left of this and make for a stile to the right of a hedge on the field boundary.

E Cross the stile heading straight across the next field to a signpost by a hedgerow.

F Turn right and follow the path with a hedge to your right. Go through a small wood then continue with the hedge to your right. The path then turns right through gap in hedge. Head across the field to a road. Turn right and follow the road. You are now on the Viking Way, the route of which is marked by a horned Viking helmet logo.

G At the end of the road bear right through a gap in the hedge, then turn left with the hedge to your left. Carry straight on following the track through a small wood to a kissing gate.

H Bear right diagonally uphill across the field. At the top go through two kissing gates separated by a footbridge. Continue uphill, following the field boundary with Belchford Wood to your right.

I When you reach a kissing gate go through it and carry straight ahead with a hedge on your right. The hill, with the trees on top, to your left is Juicetrump Hill. Continue through a gap in the hedge and go across the field then follow the hedgerow to your right.

J Turn right over a footbridge in the hedgerow and then immediately left and follow the field boundary with a hedge to your left.

K At the corner of the field go over a footbridge, through a hedge and bear left following the field boundary with the hedge to your left. Go through a kissing gate at end of field, in the next field follow the path on the left-hand side and then through another kissing gate onto the road. On the road turn left and follow the road back into the village.

View from the churchyard of St Peter and St Paul

The village of Billinghay sits on a slightly elevated ridge of sand and gravel surrounded by flat low-lying arable farmland much of which is below 30ft (10m) above sea level. This land would originally have been marshland which flooded during the winter, leaving the village as a small island. There is some interesting artwork in Billinghay including a mosaic at the junction of Fitzwilliam Place and the High Street which illustrates the history of the village.

St Michael and
All Angels Church

Billinghay

Mosaic, Billinghay

Route instructions

A Leave the car park via the one-way exit route. Turn right onto Fitzwilliam Place and follow it to its junction with High Street where to your right, you will see a mosaic which illustrates the history of the village.

1 The village of Billinghay lies in the flat lands in the southern half of Lincolnshire. This is an area dominated by a comprehensive grid of drainage channels. The Billinghay Skirth drain runs along the eastern edge of the village with the Digby Dam drain to the south. This unusual landscape is what many people think of as typical Lincolnshire countryside; it is definitely big-sky country.

B Turn right onto High Street and walk past the Ship Inn and Queen Street on the left. Take the next left onto Bridge Street.

C Turn right down Church Lane past the church. Then left at the end and continue past the War Memorial.

2 The oldest bits of St Michael and All Angels church in Billinghay date from Norman times, but it has undergone considerable rebuilding and reconstruction over the intervening centuries. In 1787 the spire was rebuilt and there was major refurbishment of the structure during Victorian times. In common with quite a number of Lincolnshire

Plan your walk

Kingston upon Hull
Scunthorpe • Immingham
Grimsby
Louth
• Lincoln
Skegness
Sleaford Boston
• Grantham The
Wash
• Spalding

DISTANCE: 2¾ miles (4.25km)

TIME: 1½ hours

START/END: TF152548 Park in the Village Hall car park

TERRAIN: Easy

MAPS:
OS Explorer 261;
OS Landranger 121

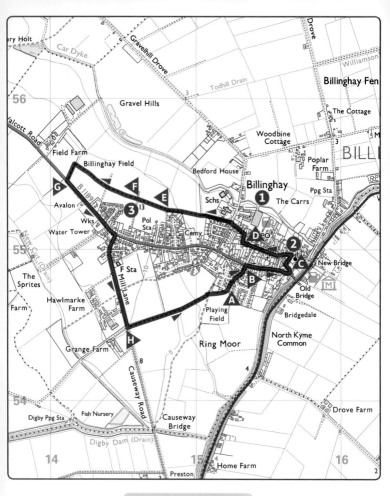

villages, the church, which seats 300 people, seems to be quite large for the community it serves.

D Follow the road as it bends sharply to the right and then turn left onto West Street. At the end of West Street cross over the road and take the footpath opposite to the left of the school. Pass through a gate, and continue until you reach an open field. Carry on walking on the left hand side of the field.

E At the end of the field go through a kissing gate, cross a private road, over a stile and then across another field towards a stile with a trig point beside it.

Billinghay

❸ To the northwest of Billinghay is a 13m triangulation point. Often called trig points, most of us think of these as being located on the tops of mountains, and many of them are, but in this low-lying area this 13m trig pillar constitutes a high point. These are usually concrete pillars with a metal plate on the top where a theodolite can be mounted. Built by the Ordnance Survey, most of the current network of trig points in Britain date from about 1935 to 1962. From each pillar, in clear weather, you can see at least two other trig points. Various measurements are then taken to these pillars, so creating a system of triangles (hence the name triangulation point) which are referred back to a carefully measured baseline.

F Then take a diagonal path across the field towards some farm buildings. The tall structure to your left is a water tower. Cross a ditch via a footbridge and through a gap in the hedge, then turn left towards the road with the hedge on your left hand side.

G At the road turn left and head back towards the village. Go past the water tower to your right and turn right onto Mill Lane. Go past the Fire Station and continue along the road ignoring a footpath on the left.

H Take the second footpath on your left opposite a road to the right signposted Digby. Continue along this path with the hedge to your left. Go through the squeeze gate onto the playing field and back to the village hall car park.

Triangulation point

...walk takes you across open fields to the pretty hamlet of Tealby Thorpe where its woodlands and then back again across open countryside and ... into Willingham Woods.

To the east of Market Rasen lie Willingham Woods. This area of coniferous and deciduous trees with streams running through to some ponds is a lovely place for a walk at all times of the year. If you are quiet, you may spot some deer who make their home here. There are also plenty of birds, insects and wild flowers to be seen. In the car park there are toilets, a refreshment kiosk (open from February to November) and a picnic site.

Fields southwest of
Tealby Thorpe

Willingham Woods & Tealby Thorpe

Ford at Tealby Thorpe

Plan your walk

DISTANCE: 3¼ miles (5.25km)

TIME: 1¾ hours

START/END: TF138884 Park in the Forestry Commission car park

TERRAIN: Easy; possibly some muddy fields

MAPS:
OS Explorer 282;
OS Landranger 113

Route instructions

A Leave the car park at the eastern end and turn left onto the footpath at the side of Willingham Road. Follow this until you reach a council depot road and turn left onto the footpath just beyond it.

B Head across a field towards the corner of a brick building, pass through a small wooded area by a stream. Cross the stream via a footbridge.

C Cross the field diagonally heading towards a clump of small trees, then cross the rest of the field and head towards a footbridge to the left of a hedgerow.

D Cross the footbridge and bear right slightly uphill across a field. At the brow

of the hill you should see a footpath sign ahead, continue towards it and turn right along a track.

E Where the track bends to the left carry straight on along the signed footpath at the side of the field with a hedge to your left. Continue to the road and then turn left. Follow the road turning left at the next junction. Continue on the road with Thorpe Farm to your left.

1 Tealby Thorpe is notable for having two fords where the River Rase flows through the hamlet. The longer of the two is quite deep and it can be more like driving across a river bed than across a road.

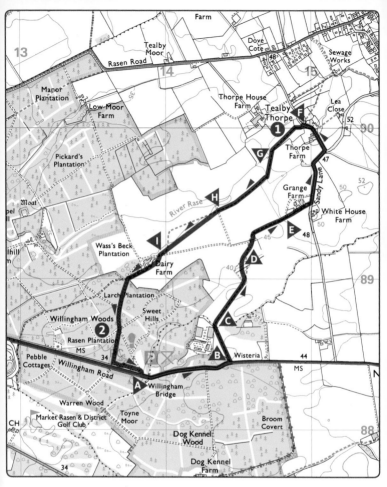

F Take the path on the left immediately before the first ford. Ignoring the footbridge to the right, follow the path signed to Willingham Woods. The path goes through a small wood to a kissing gate, then across a field to the far corner.

G Go through the kissing gate, bear right towards a footbridge. Cross this and proceed straight ahead keeping the large ash and oak trees to your left, heading for the footpath sign.

H At the signpost continue straight across the next field heading towards the buildings of 'Dairy Farm'.

Willingham Woods & Tealby Thorpe

▶ Just before the farm, cross the track, go through two kissing gates and passing to the left of the farm head towards the woods. Turn left on the forest track and follow this back to the car park.

❷ Owned by the Forestry Commission, Willingham Woods has a network of paths and tracks. The woods are mainly coniferous, with an understorey of bracken. In the more densely planted areas, so little light gets through that the forest floor is just a mat of pine needles and it can be really dark, even on the brightest days; but there are occasional patches of mixed deciduous woodland which are rich with ground flora. The River Rase, as well as several small streams, flow through the woods and there are some small ponds which are home to ducks, moorhens and coots. Much of the wildlife makes itself scarce during the busy summer months but if you visit in winter, or early in the day, you may be lucky and spot some of the locals.

Willingham Woods

> **As you walk between the villages of Folkingham, Walcot and Pickworth you cross the gently undulating countryside that separates them, and for much of the walk you can see the spires and towers of the village churches**

The villages of Folkingham, Pickworth and Walcot lie in the southern half of Lincolnshire in the gently rolling limestone hills of the Kesteven Uplands. Our walk takes us into each village via open fields, across streams and beside mixed hedgerows. This area is very much in the heart of the countryside, a world away from the hustle and bustle of everyday life. Each of the villages has an ancient church built of the local stone, each with a story to tell; they seem to stand like sentinels over their respective settlements.

St Andrew's Church, Pickworth

Folkingham

Countryside between Walcot and Pickworth

Route instructions

A Head north towards the church, go to its left and then turn left into the graveyard extension. Go through the gate onto the road. Turn right and continue north past new houses on the left and go straight ahead across the field towards a footbridge.

1 As you approach the village of Folkingham from the south and enter the market square you are confronted by the impressive red brick Queen Anne façade of the Greyhound. Just behind this to the left you see the 15th century tower of St Andrew's church. Inside the church are some interesting artefacts of historical village life, such as the old whipping post and stocks. From the early 17th to the early 20th century, the village was an important legal centre and these items are relics of this time. It was the seat of the 'Quarter Sessions' which were a high court responsible for administering justice in the local area.

B Cross the footbridge and head across the field towards a tree, then bear left across the next field.

C Cross the footbridge and continue, bearing left towards a hedgerow. At the edge of the field cross another footbridge and bear left across the next field towards a stile in the hedge.

Plan your walk

- Kingston upon Hull
- Scunthorpe • Immingham
  - Grimsby
  - Louth
- Lincoln
  - Skegness
  - Sleaford • Boston
- Grantham • The Wash
  - Spalding

DISTANCE: 5 miles (8km)

TIME: 3 hours

START/END: TF072337 Park in Market Place in Folkingham

TERRAIN: Easy

MAPS:
OS Explorer 248;
OS Landranger 130

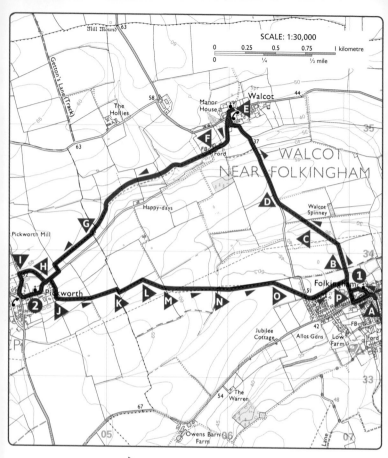

D Cross the stile and turn right onto the road. Continue towards the village of Walcot. Keep right and cross over Village Street to the church of St Nicholas.

E From the church, cross back over the road bearing right down a road signed 'Pickworth'.

F Just before a ford turn right over a stile into a field, and follow the path with the hedge to your left. Continue in a generally south-westerly direction following waymarks with a stream to your left. Cross three fields via stiles and footbridges.

G Cross a stile through a hedge and continue on the left-hand side of a field in the direction of Pickworth church. At the field's end turn left to the road then right into Pickworth.

Folkingham

H Turn right onto the footpath opposite the road called Church Fields. Then cross a field to a footbridge, cross this and follow the left-hand side of the field to the road.

I Turn left on the road keeping left at the first junction and turning left at the second junction onto Church Lane. Pass St Andrew's church to your left, and take the footpath on the right just past Church Fields. Continue between the houses to a stile.

2 The medieval church of St Andrew's in Pickworth has some fascinating 14th century paintings illustrating, amongst other things, some biblical scenes and a few fairly gruesome moral images such as three people in a cauldron. Around about the mid 16th century the paintings were whitewashed over and hidden, but they revealed themselves during World War II when a bomb exploded nearby. The vibrations from the blast knocked off some of the plaster and paint thus exposing parts of the images.

J Head diagonally uphill across the field to the corner. Go over a stile and bear slightly right across the next field to the far side.

K Turn right in front of a hedge. Continue for approximately 30 yards (30m) and then turn left over a footbridge. Continue straight ahead with a hedge on your left.

L Approximately two-thirds of the way along the field look for a waymarked post and then bear right across the field towards a footbridge. Then continue bearing left to a hedgerow.

M Cross a footbridge at a hedgerow and bear right across the next field in the direction of Folkingham church tower.

N Cross another footbridge and continue straight ahead with the hedge to your left.

O At a waymark post about three quarters of the way along the field, bear right to a high fence on the far side. Go through a gate in the fence, bear right and head towards the far corner of the playing field. Pass through a gate, cross the road and turn into Wilkie Drive. As it bends to the left take the footpath straight ahead between fences.

P Turn right with the church and rectory on your left and follow the driveway to the road where you turn left back to Market Place and the car.

66 You should be rewarded with the sights and sounds of an array of wildlife as you stroll through Snipe Dales Nature Reserve and Country Park and into the rolling countryside to the east **99**

This lovely area in the south of the Lincolnshire Wolds is a wildlife haven. There are valleys, ponds, marshy areas and rough grazing land as well as both deciduous and coniferous trees. The diversity of habitat makes for quite an array of birdlife. If you are lucky you may spot the tiny goldcrest flitting amongst the trees or, at dusk, the beautiful barn owl may make an appearance. In the reserve and country park nine newly-dug ponds have been quickly colonised and have already proved popular with migrant waders and waterfowl as well as various amphibians and insects.

Snipe Dales & Winceby

Battle of Winceby
memorial stone

Route instructions

A Leave the car park and turn left onto the main road passing Winceby House Farm. On the grass verge is a memorial to the Battle of Winceby.

1 Although the Battle of Winceby, which took place on 11th October 1643, is one of the smaller battles of the English Civil War it is considered of great significance in the overall outcome of the war. Up until this point the Royalists had been very much in the ascendancy, but at Winceby, Cromwell and Sir Thomas Fairfax fought side by side for the first time and gave the Parliamentarian cavalry their first significant victory. This was the starting point of a change in the tide of the war.

B Past the entrance to Winceby House turn left, cross a stile and follow the left-hand side of the field. Cut across the corner of the field bearing right towards a stile.

C Enter the nature reserve and follow the path with the fence to your left. Cross a stile and walk downhill. Go through a gate.

2 The 220 acre (89ha) Snipe Dales Country Park and Nature Reserve comprises two steep-sided valleys fed by a series of small streams. The geology of porous sand overlying impervious clay has led to the creation of numerous spring-fed streams which emerge where the two

Plan your walk

DISTANCE: 4¼ miles (7km)

TIME: 2½ hours

START/END: TF319682 Park in Snipe Dales Nature Reserve car park (NB no dogs allowed in the nature reserve)

TERRAIN: Moderate

MAPS:
OS Explorer 273;
OS Landranger 122

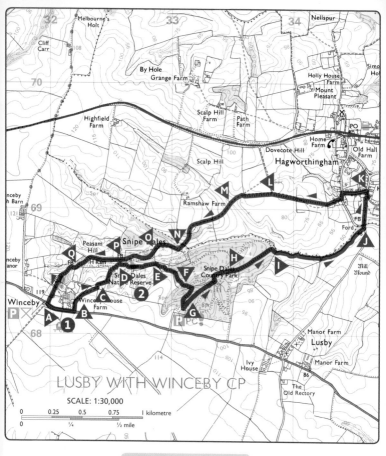

rocks meet. Over the last few decades ponds have been excavated, mixed deciduous woodland planted and the grassland grazed by livestock to encourage plants that thrive in short turf. This has led to a huge improvement in the diversity of the flora and fauna, with plenty to see at any time of the year.

D Turn right at a red waymarked post BEFORE reaching a footbridge. Cross a stream via a wide bridge and head uphill.

E Go through a gate, follow the path bearing right heading towards pine wood.

F Enter the woodland, bear right following red markers along a track and then head downhill signed 'country park car park'. Turn right over a footbridge and walk uphill to the car park.

Snipe Dales & Winceby

G Turn left and head downhill to the right of the buildings. At the bottom, turn right and then first left over a footbridge and then turn right and continue along the path with river to your right. At a junction of paths turn right and follow track.

H At a cross roads in the track go straight ahead signed Bolingbroke Way/ Snipe Dales Round.

I Follow sign to Hagworthingham, go over a footbridge to your right, then over a stile. Follow the path on the left-hand side of the field, through a kissing gate until you reach a road.

J Cross the road with a ford to your left and enter Furze Hill Nature Reserve. Bear left and cross footbridge then bear right uphill across field heading towards a house. Cross stile and follow path between fence and hedge and then over another stile turning left onto a track into Hagworthingham.

K At the road turn left and head downhill turning left at the junction. Soon after, turn right through a gate onto a footpath just before Woodside Cottage. Follow this until you reach a field. Cross field diagonally uphill to the right to a gap in the hedge.

L Where the path meets a track continue until it bends to the right. Take the path straight on through silver birch trees, downhill and turn left.

M Cross footbridge and head straight on up the slope to a signpost at a gap in the hedge. There is a modern stone circle to your right. Follow the path as it curves across the field to the left towards a gate.

N Go through the gate, head downhill through a small wood, across a small field and over a footbridge into the nature reserve. Continue up a short hill and with a fence ahead of you, turn right at the path junction. Follow the path with valley to your left.

O Go through a gate and head downhill bending to the right with the stream to your left.

P Ignoring the footbridge to your left continue straight on with the stream to your left. At the water ram bear left, head uphill, through a gate and follow a track.

Q Cross the footbridge and follow the path past St Margaret's graveyard. Cross a stile, turn left and follow the track back to the car park.

> 66 Passing through the lovely countryside to the east of Old Bolingbroke this walk takes in some superb far-reaching views and visits the ruins of the 13th-century castle which was the birthplace of Henry IV, the first Lancastrian king 99

The little village of Old Bolingbroke to the southeast of Horncastle has two main claims to fame: the castle, now a ruin, was the birthplace of Henry IV, the first of the Lancastrian kings; and it also played an important role as a garrison for the Royalists during the English Civil War of the mid 17th century. Originally just called Bolingbroke, the village was renamed when New Bolingbroke was built a few miles to the southwest in the early 19th century with market rights transferring to the new settlement.

Countryside to the east of
Old Bolingbroke

Old Bolingbroke

St Peter and St Paul Church

Plan your walk

Kingston upon Hull
Scunthorpe • Immingham
• Grimsby
• Louth
• Lincoln
Skegness
Sleaford • Boston
Grantham The Wash
• Spalding

DISTANCE: 4¼ miles (7km)

TIME: 2½ hours

START/END: TF349652 Park beside the church in Old Bolingbroke

TERRAIN: Moderate; some hills

MAPS:
OS Explorer 273;
OS Landranger 122

Route instructions

A With your back to the church turn right and walk up the road heading east. At the junction signed 'Spilsby', turn left. Continue uphill and just before the village sign turn right at the 'Hundleby' sign and go through a kissing gate. Follow the path uphill with hedge and fence to your right to a kissing gate, there are good views of the surrounding countryside from here. Bear slightly right across the field heading for a gate.

1 Originally just called Bolingbroke, its name changed after a new village was built to the south with the same name, taking the market rights with it; as a result, we now have Old Bolingbroke and New Bolingbroke. Henry IV's association with the village is commemorated with his coat of arms in the middle of a flower bed of red Lancastrian roses which is located in the heart of the village.

B Bear right through a gap between a hedge and fence and continue with the hedge on your left. Follow the path across the field.

C At the footpath post bear right across the field to the corner and go through a gap in the hedge. Then bear left across a field to a stile.

D Cross the stile and go over a footbridge and continue straight uphill across the field.

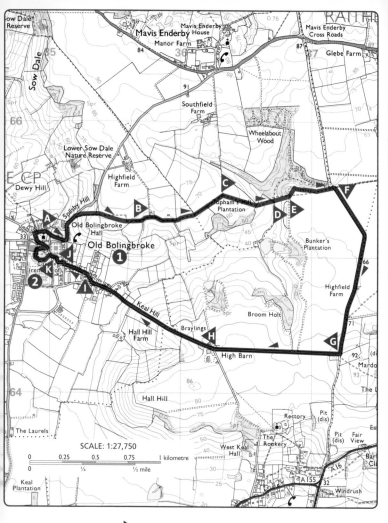

E Go through a gap in the trees following the waymark across a field bearing left and then right beside the field edge until you reach the road.

F Turn right and follow the road. Continue straight on

at the junction heading for 'West Keal' and 'Stickford'. From here the road climbs slightly uphill.

G Turn right at the junction signed 'Old Bolingbroke' and head along the road where there are excellent

Old Bolingbroke

views to north and south. To the south you should see the tower of West Keal church and, just to the left of this in the far distance, on a clear day you may be able to see the Boston Stump.

H▶ Continue on the road signed Old Bolingbroke and follow it downhill into the village.

I▶ When you reach the village follow the road to the right signed 'Mavis Enderby' and 'Hareby'.

J▶ At the end of the road turn right and immediately left into the lane almost opposite. The lane bends to the right and then the left, and then straight ahead of you is the entrance gate to the castle.

K▶ Enter the gate to the castle ruins, look around and leave by the northern exit to the right of the small building. Turn left on the road, past the Black Horse Inn on the right and turn right back to the start point.

2 Bolingbroke Castle was built around 1220 by Randulph de Blundeville, Earl of Chester and Lincoln. It was built with a wide moat and it had five towers and a gatehouse. Eventually the castle passed into the ownership of Edward III's fourth son John of Gaunt,

Duke of Lancaster (via a rather circuitous route through his wife Blanche). Their son, often referred to as Henry Bolingbroke, was born here in 1367 and went on to seize the throne from Richard II in 1399, so becoming Henry IV.

The castle was also used as a garrison during the Civil War and this proved to be its undoing. With the Parliamentarians' victory and the setting up of the Commonwealth under Cromwell, there was a fear that castles such as this could be used as strongholds for rebellion, so, in 1652 it was destroyed. Today the castle, which is open to visitors all year round and is free of charge, remains a ruin, but the shape of the castle can be clearly seen; parts of the curtain wall stand to a height of about 18ft (6m).

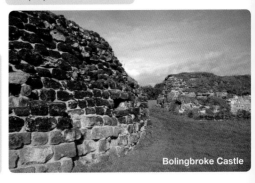
Bolingbroke Castle

66 With views of the Boston Stump along the way this walk is fairly long, but flat, and takes in the water courses of Hobhole Drain and The Haven as well as the little village of Fishtoft **99**

Not far from Boston and a few miles inland from The Wash coastline is Fishtoft. The village sits between The Haven and Hobhole Drain. These water courses provide a rich environment for wildlife, particularly birds. On the muddy banks of The Haven you frequently see dunlin, a multitude of gulls, oystercatchers and redshanks; and along the Hobhole Drain you may see ducks, coots and grebes. This whole area is extremely low lying and is criss-crossed by man-made drainage channels; the village sits on some glacial clays which form a slightly higher area of ground surrounded by the lower lying river sediments.

Fishtoft

Field near Fishtoft

Route instructions

▶ Starting at the car park head south towards the Pilgrim Fathers Memorial, cross the stile to the left of the memorial. Follow path along an embankment, then over a stile, through an area of scrub and down some steps. Turn left to follow Hobhole Drain on its left-hand bank. This path has a hawthorn hedge to the right and open fields to the left of you. Eventually the fields on the left give way to a hedgerow and you enter Hobhole Bank Nature Reserve.

1 A granite memorial to the Pilgrim Fathers, can be seen just to the northwest of the junction between The Haven and Hobhole Drain. The memorial was erected in 1957 in memory of a group of Puritan pilgrims, later known as the Pilgrim Fathers, who set sail in September 1607 on their first attempt at finding religious freedom across the seas in Holland. However, leaving the country without permission was illegal at that time and their bid for freedom failed when the captain of the Dutch boat they chartered betrayed them. They were arrested and imprisoned in nearby Boston.

A successful attempt to get to Holland was made the following year from the Humber. Then, in 1620 they finally made the historic trip to set up a colony in the New World when they set sail from Plymouth in the *Mayflower*.

Plan your walk

Kingston upon Hull
Scunthorpe • Immingham
• Grimsby
• Louth
• Lincoln
• Skegness
• Sleaford • Boston
• Grantham The Wash
• Spalding

DISTANCE: 5 miles (8km)

TIME: 3 hours

START/END: TF360402 Car park near Pilgrim Fathers Memorial by The Haven

TERRAIN: Easy

MAPS:
OS Explorer 261;
OS Landranger 131

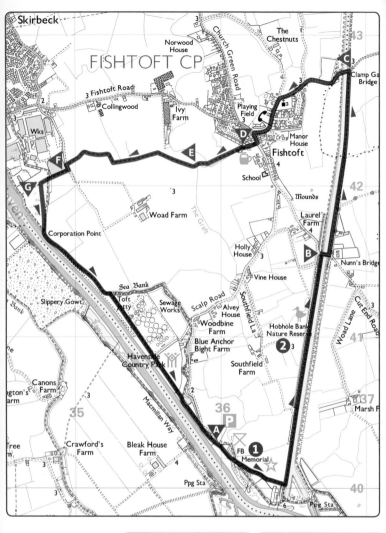

2 Lying on the western bank of the Hobhole Drain is the 12.4 acre (5ha) Hobhole Bank Nature Reserve comprising mainly of rough grassland, elder, hawthorn and willow. A variety of birds call the reserve home and in winter large numbers of thrushes and finches can sometimes be seen roosting in the trees and shrubs. In spring the grassland is awash with cowslips which make a fantastic show. On the Drain

Fishtoft

there are plenty of water birds to see all year round including various ducks as well as grebes and herons.

B Upon emerging from the nature reserve you reach a road where you turn right, over Nunn's Bridge then left to follow the east side of the drain.

C Continue until you reach a pillbox. Turn left across Clamp Gate Bridge and then follow the road into the village of Fishtoft, passing the church of St Guthlac on your left.

D Turn left into Gaysfield Road in front of the Red Cow Inn. Soon after the pub car park turn right down Old School Lane. At the end of the road turn right, then immediately left with the allotments on your right and hedge on your left. The path emerges onto open fields. Follow the path with the ditch to your left across the field. You may see the Boston Stump in the distance to your right. Continue on, keeping the ditch to your left until you reach a painted post.

E At the post, turn right keeping the small ditch to your right. You are heading in the general direction of a large warehouse in the distance. Continue to a road.

F At the road, with the warehouse in front of you, turn left and then right to follow a footpath along the side of the warehouse. Cross a small bridge and then go up some steps. You are now entering Havenside Nature Reserve.

G At a four-way footpath signpost, turn left. Turn left again where the path meets The Haven and continue on the path with The Haven channel to your right. Go through a metal gate, then past the sewage works and then through another gate. Follow the path back to the car park.

Sunflower field near the Hobhole Drain

Photo credits

All photographs © HarperCollins Publishers Ltd,
photographers Helen Gordon and Richard Knight,
with the exception of:

Page 27: © Ana del Castillo /
Shutterstock images